CRICKET

SECRET CHILD OF A
SIXTIES SUPERMODEL

SUSAN FEDORKO

outskirtspress
DENVER, COLORADO

For my loving family

Cathee Dahmen photographed by Neal Barr for Bazaar Cover 1968

"I see all of us in you."

Elaine Dahmen Colbert

Table of Contents

Preface i

Questions 1
Chapter 1:   The Call (Part 1) 3
Chapter 2:   *Cathee* / Cricket / Susie 9
Chapter 3:   School Girl / Fashion Model.................. 20
Chapter 4:   Party Girl / *Celebrity Wife* 33
Chapter 5:   Love / Marriage 46
Chapter 6:   Samantha / Sasha 52
Chapter 7:   Hard Times / Good Times 59

Answers 77
Chapter 8:   The Call (Part 2) 79
Chapter 9:   Cathee's Children................................ 100
Chapter 10:   Tommy's Children 105
Chapter 11:   White Earth Nation 114
Chapter 12:   Grand Portage Nation 117
Chapter 13:   Cathee's New York 123
Chapter 14:   Rendezvous 130
Chapter 15:   Aftermath.. 139

Appendix A: Timeline 151
Appendix B: Hangover Soup 157

- Disclaimer: some family names and identifying details have been changed.

Susie & Tim Fedorko May 2001

Preface

I was found on November 25, 2002. That's not to say I'd been lost. But I sure was in limbo.

I've known since the age of five that I was adopted. I've also known since childhood that I'm Native American. What I learned about my birth mother when I turned eighteen was sketchy at best. I knew even less about my birth father. But in 2002, the year I turned forty, I wanted—I needed—to know more about them so I could know more about me.

So I posted my meager birth history on an adoption website, asking for any information about my biological family. The woman who responded on that November day ten years ago had seen my plea and put two and two together. That woman was, in fact, my half-sister, Sarah, and what she told me then still astonishes me now: she said that our mother, Cathee Dahmen, had been an international fashion model, that she had had two celebrity marriages, and that her uncle was the famed Native American impressionist painter George Morrison. Those discoveries eventually led to several others, including the identity of my birth father, Tom Conklin, and five more half-siblings, not to mention scores of aunts, uncles, and cousins on both sides of my birth families.

Since that remarkable day in 2002, I've been trying to sort out how I can create new family bonds without cutting old family ties.

From the start, my intention in writing this memoir has been simple: to document my journey so that everyone in my extended family— my adoptive family, my birth family, my husband and daughters—will have a better idea of who I was "before," who I have become "after," and how and why it all happened.

The journey has not been easy. I've had to take the bitter with the sweet. I've exchanged e-mails, for example, with my birth mother's ex-husbands, asking each to tell me about their lives with her. One shared a little information, and the other made it clear that he wanted nothing to do with me. Neither wanted his name mentioned in this or any other book I might write.

Well, I *struggled* with mentioning their names in this book. Cathee Dahmen was a public figure, and her marriages are a matter of public record. Her ex-husbands are part of her life story and, therefore, part of mine. I am not mentioning some family by legal name at their request. I have only mentioned Sarah Knestrick, my beautiful half sister who found me. Sarah is not ashamed of me and wants me to tell my story to whomever I want to. But my memoir isn't about them. It's about me and my life before and after my half-sister found me. I'm not looking to write an exposé about my birth mother's ex-husbands, or anyone else for that matter. I'm not looking for money or a new dad. I'm looking to know more about the young woman who gave me up for adoption two weeks before my first birthday. I'm asking her ex-husbands and others who knew her for the answers to my questions because I can't. She died before I was found. So did my birth father.

For the mistakes I may have made in telling my story, I apologize. This is my disclaimer. They are unintentional. They are also inevitable, I suppose. After all, the events surrounding my birth took place fifty years ago. The key witnesses to those events aren't here to speak for themselves. But I believe that the people who knew my birth parents best have done their best in recalling the truth of those times. And I am thankful for their help.

I owe thanks to my many Dahmen and Conklin relatives who helped me to connect the dots of my identity to theirs. In particular,

I'm grateful to my half sister Sarah Knestrick for having the heart and the strength to reach out to find me. It must have been a huge gamble for her, not knowing how I would react to being located after so many years. But I grasped her hand with both of mine and have not regretted one moment of getting to know her and the rest of my birth mother's family.

I also owe much to two of my birth mother's sisters, Elaine Dahmen Colbert and Barbara Dahmen. In some ways Elaine took my birth mother's place and held my hand during the first years of this challenging process. Barb took up where Elaine left off. Both aunts, pillars of my newfound family, died as I was writing this memoir.

I'm grateful to Evie Conklin Shew, my birth father's half sister, for reaching out to find me on behalf of my Conklin relatives, and to Nellie Cadue, my birth father's first wife, for generously sharing details about my birth father as a younger man.

Special thanks to Neal Barr, Helmut Newton and Elle magazine, all who have allowed me permission to use their professional photographs of my birth mother. Without these images it would be impossible to imagine just how beautiful Cathee was. Thanks also to my birth mother's contemporaries for sharing their memories of Cathee: Linda Morand, fashion model and creator of the Supermodels Hall of Fame; Patty Sicular; Bill Cunningham, street fashion photographer and New York acquaintance; James Michael Lawrence, artist and Minneapolis classmate; and Lou Mendelsohn, financial software pioneer and Rhode Island confidante who filled in critical blanks in my birth mother's story—and mine. I am also thankful to Travis Novitsky of Grand Portage for his beautiful photo of the spirit tree. Thanks to Steve Glaser Photo Rescue & Graphics for the majority of my pictures and cover design. Cover photo of Cathee Dahmen by Neal Barr for Harper's Bazaar, May 1968. Thanks Neal Barr!

Thanks also to my friend and former coworker Eric Keene, who listened and understood as only a fellow adoptee could, and to my manuscript editor, Michele Hodgson, who helped me put my feelings and thoughts into words that expressed what I needed and wanted to say.

No words can describe how deeply indebted I am to Lloyd and Virginia Smith, my adoptive father and mother. They have loved me and cared for me and molded me into the person I am today. I could not have asked for better parents. I also want to acknowledge my Smith siblings, Stephen and Connie. We don't always see eye to eye, but whatever our differences, we are family.

Finally, I am beyond grateful to my husband, Tim, and our daughters, Samantha and Sasha. They have stood by me as I wept tears of joy and sorrow over the past ten years, even as I was becoming someone other than the wife and mother they had always known. I have had life-changing moments, both good and sad, and they have stood by my side for all of them. Without their continuing love and patience, I never could have taken this journey let alone survived it. Tim in particular has been my rock, the love of my life, who has helped me overcome every obstacle and make my every dream come true. Thanks Tim!

Tim Fedorko 2012

Questions

CHAPTER 1

The Call (Part 1)

More often than not, when I would fantasize about how my birth mother and I might meet, I imagined it to be a simple but perfect reunion: she'd knock on my front door, give me a smile as big as my own, and tell me the answers to all of the questions I had ever had about us.

I tried to find my birth mother back when I was eighteen, but nothing much came of it, other than a three-page genetic history that the adoption agency sent to me. The typewritten document gave me the bare facts: when and where I was born, what my ethnic background was, what my birth parents looked like, and why my birth mother put me up for adoption. The report gave no names, no contact information, no identifying details that would help me find either parent or their families. That's the deal in closed-adoption states like Minnesota: I had to wait for them to find me, not the other way around. As the years passed, and as I turned thirty and then forty without a word from either birth family, I nearly gave up on ever hearing from them.

All of that changed at 8:00 a.m. on November 25, 2002. I was getting settled at my desk at work in downtown Minneapolis. It was going to be a busy week, and a short one at that, because of the long Thanksgiving weekend coming up. My plan for that Monday morning was to finish my last-minute preparations before giving a software training presentation at 8:30 to several staffing coworkers. But first I listened to my voice mail to clear messages left over from the previous Friday afternoon. I grabbed a cup of black coffee from the break room, set it next to my phone, and heard a message that stopped me cold:

Hi, Susan. My name is Sarah, and this message is probably going to sound very bizarre to you. I am actually looking for . . . a Susan Fedorko, who was . . . adopted and who would be forty years old now. If you are that person, I would love to hear from you. My number is 914 xxx-xxxx. And please (giggle) don't think I am nuts. If you're not that person, would you please . . . just . . . give me a call back . . . to let me know that you're not, so I won't be anticipating . . . Anyway, if it is you, I look forward to hearing from you . . . and hope to hear from you soon.

It's almost impossible to describe how dazed I felt when I heard Sarah's message, and yet my mind was racing. Whose voice was this? Was it my birth mother's? Was it her sister's, the one my adoption agency had said babysat me while my birth mother went to high school? The most likely relative to come looking for me? Did the voice have her facts right? Was she really looking for *me*?

I was so rattled I couldn't remember how to save the message, let alone memorize it. Our office had just installed new phones, and I was unfamiliar with operating them. What if I hit the wrong button and erased the message, never to be contacted by the voice again? Panicked, I called out to my coworker Bruce to help me save the message while pleading with him to be careful not to delete it.

I looked at my watch. The training session was supposed to start in less than thirty minutes. But how could I concentrate on teaching a software program? My mind was mush. I thought about canceling the training, then doubted that my supervisor would see my distress as an acceptable excuse. Instead I told my officemates whose desks were closest to mine that we'd briefly postpone. I sent a e-mail message to the rest of the staff to say that I was delaying the training session for an hour due to a personal emergency.

Bruce and I pulled out the phone book to look up Sarah's area code. If I knew what part of the country she was calling from, maybe I could get a preliminary handle on who she was and what she was like. If she were calling from California, for instance, I could expect a laid-back resident of the West Coast. But Sarah was calling from New York. *New York!* I had yearned to visit the city for as long as I could remember. I was about to find out why.

I stared at the phone, arms and hands heavy, not moving. After fifteen minutes, I dialed the number using a prepaid phone card. The sweet voice that answered belonged to Sarah. When I told her who I was, she asked me a few more questions: Are you the Susan Fedorko who was adopted? Were you born June 23, 1962, in St. Paul, Minnesota? Did you post an entry on the adoption search board? I wanted to answer yes to her questions with more assurance in my voice, but it turned weak with the worry that eventually I'd have to answer no. That didn't happen. With each hesitant yes, I knew that my birth family had found me after all these years.

I asked her, "Are you the sister?"—meaning my birth mother's older sister—and Sarah said yes. I began to cry.

She then said she was sorry to have to tell me this, but my birth mother had died five years ago to the day, November 25, 1997. The words barely had a chance to sink in before she asked whether I knew who my birth mother was. No, I said. I had no name, no details, just a basic family background. I could barely comprehend what she said next.

Sarah told me that my birth mother was Cathee Dahmen, a *huge* model who had been photographed for top fashion magazines. At first I was confused; I thought "huge" meant that she was a model for Lane Bryant and other plus-size labels. Then Sarah explained that Cathee had been featured in *Vogue, Harper's Bazaar, Elle,* and other high-fashion magazines. With obvious admiration, Sarah quickly filled me in on just how successful Cathee had been as a professional model. She had posed for the likes of David Bailey, Antonio Lopez, and other well-known photographers and illustrators. She had worked for the

Eileen Ford Agency. Sarah also said Cathee's first husband was British actor Leroy Winter. Her second husband was Adam Merrick, lead singer and bass guitarist for a British band.

But not until Sarah said that "Mom" had two other children, Lana and Adam Jr., with her second husband did it dawn on me: Sarah wasn't my aunt. She was my half-sister!

Sarah talked a bit about the large Minnesota family Cathee had come from and told me the names of aunts and uncles. She asked, timidly, if I wanted to know the name of my birth father. She confessed that she knew very little about him, other than that his name was Tommy Conklin.

As she talked, Sarah dropped so many names so fast that it overwhelmed me. I didn't recognize any of them. I had no clue who they were. And I still had no idea just how famous Cathee was. For now all I could think was *the mystery is over. I have the names of my birth parents.*

Sarah and I talked for no more than fifteen minutes. We could have spent hours more on the phone, but I had that damned presentation to give. We agreed that she would call me after I got home from work and also try to set up a conference call to include our half-sister, Lana. Meanwhile we exchanged e-mail addresses so we could send each other photos of ourselves and our families. She also gave me her web page address so I could see pictures of Cathee and her family. Sarah's photos arrived before the training session began, but they were saved in a format that was incompatible with my government computer. I had no luck converting the file either. I finally sent it to my home e-mail to open it there. That meant I would have to wait until four o'clock to see them. *I thought how the hell was I going to last till then?*

For the rest of the workday, I couldn't concentrate on anything—phone calls, technical questions, and least of all my presentation. All I wanted was to get home, perch next to the phone, and wait for Sarah to call again. But I hung in there and got through it, thanks to an understanding staff who had already heard rumblings of my news.

I knew I wouldn't be able to hold it together during the training session, so I briefly told them what had just happened to me.

And what exactly *had* happened? As I drove home, my mind kept replaying my conversation with Sarah, trying to make sense of it. How surreal that this stranger knew more about me than I did. Thanks to her, I had more facts about my birth parents than before. But facts tell only part of the story. They tell you *what* but not always *why*.

And that's when the realization that Cathee was dead really sunk in. My fantasies of seeing her, listening to her, and having long conversations with her would never become reality. I'd never hear her tell me to my face why she gave me up. I'd never be able to ask her why she had not looked for me. Maybe with a little detective work I could locate my birth father and ask him the questions I'd never be able to ask Cathee. But could Tommy Conklin tell me more about Cathee? Would he want to see me or have a relationship with me or my daughters? Would he even want to know that I exist? Was he dead too?

I comforted myself with the idea that even though she was gone, I could talk to Cathee's spirit at any time, now that I knew her name. I'm not a go-to-church-every-Sunday kind of Catholic, but my faith is strong, and I believe in an afterlife. I had not known till today that her spirit had left this world five years ago, but I had the sense that Cathee had probably been watching over me since then. She could see who I was and who I had become.

Once I was home, I tore through boxes and piles of papers until I found the three-page genetic history the adoption agency had written up at the time of my birth. As I reread it, I wondered how Cathee's life could have changed so dramatically in such a short time. How does a scared, unwed teen who gives up her baby for adoption turn into a confident supermodel who marries a movie star and a rock musician?

I sat and waited by the phone for Sarah's second call. I tried to scribble down more questions to ask her, but my mind kept drifting. Would my life change dramatically too, now that I had been found? Was I ready if it did? For forty years I'd been known and loved as the adopted daughter of Lloyd and Virginia Smith. For twenty of those years I'd been a happily married mother of two. I wanted those parts of my life to stay the same. But I desperately wanted to know everything I could about my other life—the life I had and then lost as the daughter of a half-Native American Minnesota teen named Cathee Dahmen.

CHAPTER 2

Cathee / Cricket / Susie

Tom Conklin & Catherine Dahmen
Susie's biological parents

Cathee Dahmen was both beautiful and artistic in the early 1960s when she was a student at Minneapolis Vocational High School. She was of average height and slim—five feet six and 109 pounds—and a striking brunette. She had deep brown eyes and a smooth olive complexion that set her apart from her blond and fair-skinned Scandinavian classmates. She was a shy but pleasant girl who applied herself well to her studies, especially her art classes. But because she was Native American—her father was German, but her mother was Chippewa—Catherine Helen Dahmen was automatically labeled trouble by her teachers and classmates.

Smoking cigarettes and pot didn't improve that perception. Neither did getting pregnant in the fall of 1961, her junior year. Back then, unwed teenage mothers were ostracized and not just in school. Teen pregnancy cast shame upon the family too, regardless of social status or religion. Girls who got into that kind of trouble would often leave town suddenly, supposedly to live with some aunt somewhere for some vague reason, only to wait out their pregnancies in homes for unwed mothers and then give up their babies for adoption. Birth control was hit or miss back then, the "Pill" still being relatively new. Abortion was rarely an option.

Cathee was less worried about her reputation and more concerned about how she could raise her baby and still make something of herself. The baby's father apparently wasn't going to be part of the solution. Tommy Conklin was a year and a half older than Cathee, a good-looking young man who played basketball and football in high school. He was born on March 13, 1944, on the White Earth Indian Reservation in northwestern Minnesota. Tommy knew about Cathee's pregnancy. In fact, they saw each other up until her fifth month or so. I'm not sure why they broke up and probably never will. Maybe Tommy was scared of the responsibility of becoming a father at the early age of eighteen. He and his two half siblings had lived in foster care. Perhaps having that experience had shown him the harsher realities of caring for children.

Cathee's parents wouldn't be of much help either. Her mother, Mary Madeline (Morrison) Dahmen, had her hands full raising her own kids. Cathee was the fifth of Mary's nine children, born September 16, 1945, in Mille Lacs County, Minnesota. She had four older sisters; one younger sister; and three younger brothers. Their father, Leo Peter Dahmen, was an uneducated, often unemployed German laborer who had grown up on a farm in Morrison County, Minnesota. To put food on the table, Leo sometimes hunted for game. On other occasions the family simply went without big meals.

During Cathee's pregnancy, her folks were separated—again—and four younger siblings were still living at home. She could see how her older sisters, some already into their second pregnancies, struggled as unwed mothers. She didn't want that kind of life for herself. She talked with them about the possibilities of adoption while she was in the last three months of her pregnancy. By then Cathee had already dropped out of eleventh grade at Minneapolis Vocational High and moved into the Catholic Maternity Home for unwed mothers in St. Paul. She continued her schooling there until Saturday, June 23, 1962.

The day was momentous for two reasons: a hailstorm hit St. Paul with golf ball-sized chunks that shattered the glass panels of the historic Como Conservatory. It was also the day that sixteen-year-old Cathee Dahmen gave birth to her baby girl at St. Joseph's Hospital, also in St. Paul.

That baby girl was me.

Cricket

Cathee christened me Veronica Rose but called me Cricket, supposedly because of some funny noise I made—maybe when I hiccupped or my tummy gurgled? I was healthy but small, weighing five pounds, nine ounces, so I stayed in the hospital for a while before I was released to the nursery at the Catholic Maternity Home.

I have no idea if Cathee's labor was difficult or who might have been present in the delivery room for support. I do know that she struggled over whether she should raise me herself, no matter how hard it would be financially, or to leave it up to adoptive parents who could love and nurture me without worrying about the cost. It could not have been an easy decision for a girl of sixteen. Ultimately Cathee decided she would not part with me. But she was also adamant about making a success of her life. So she moved in with her older sister, Marie, a married mother of two, and returned to high school to finish her education while Marie watched the baby.

Tommy and Cathee did see each other one last time—at his mother's funeral in December 1962. She died of cancer at age sixty-two.

I was six months old at the time. Cathee and her older sister, Elaine, sat at the back of the church at the funeral. I have to believe that at some point during the service, Tommy and Cathee talked about me and their future together. But nothing came of it.

Telling this next part of the story accurately is difficult because there's more than one version. One version says that Cathee's mother simply packed me up one day and surrendered me to county welfare authorities without her daughter's knowledge or permission. Apparently Mary Dahmen believed that great things were in store for her daughter, and being a single parent would only jeopardize her future success. Another version says that Cathee herself decided to give me up essentially for the same reason: I was standing in the way of her dreams.

Either way, on June 11, 1963, two weeks before my first birthday, my legal guardianship was transferred from Cathee to the commissioner of public welfare.

Soon Cathee's family arranged for her to move to Providence, Rhode Island, to live with her mother's brother, George Morrison, and his wife, Hazel. Whether Cathee's mother had already discussed this arrangement with George before I was surrendered is unclear. But moving two thousand miles away from Minnesota would allow her to make a fresh start.

George and Hazel welcomed Cathee into their home. Both were artists; George had already achieved international fame as an abstract expressionist painter and sculptor. Their only expectation was that Cathee finish school. She was a quiet and reclusive student at Hope High. Her closest friend was Lou Mendelsohn, a classmate three years younger than Cathee. After school, she stretched canvases for George and Hazel, helped prepare meals for them, and babysat their two-year-old son, Briand. Cathee spent her free time sketching, reading, and writing poetry on the second floor of Cole Farm, their eighteenth-century Colonial farmhouse.

After graduating in January 1966, Cathee took classes at the Rhode Island School of Design, where her uncle taught. Although she had no modeling experience, she also sat as a portrait model for some of George's artist friends. One of her portraits caught the eye of fashion illustrator Antonio Lopez, a native Puerto Rican who lived and worked in New York City. Lopez promised Cathee that he would help launch her professional modeling career, so that spring she moved into an apartment above Carnegie Hall with Lopez and his partner, Juan Ramos. Both men began sketching her for their fashion illustrations in the *New York Times*. Street fashion photographer Bill Cunningham, who lived in the same building as the trio, remembers her as an extremely shy but down-to-earth young woman.

Just as Cathee was breaking into the world of modeling, I was making my transition from foster child to adoptee—from life as Veronica Rose Dahmen to Susan Clare Smith.

Of course, I knew nothing of Cathee Dahmen until many years later.

Susie

My adoptive parents, Lloyd Jerome Smith and Virginia Mary Reese, met during World War II in Washington, DC, where he was stationed in the Army and she worked as a secretary. Virginia lived in Waubay and Watertown, South Dakota, before moving to DC. Lloyd hailed from Glen Carbon, Illinois. They paired up at a military dance social during a singles "shoe dance." Each woman took off one of her shoes and placed it in a circle of other shoes on the dance floor. Each man picked out a shoe and went in search of the lady it belonged to, and then he danced with her the rest of the night. Lloyd picked out Virginia's shoe.

They dated for several months, then corresponded for at least a year after Lloyd was deployed overseas. My mother still has all the telegraph letters Dad sent to her, about fifty of them. He genuinely loved her but said he would understand if she began seeing someone else, referring to that imaginary someone as "the lucky stiff." Despite the distance, they remained devoted to each other and were married September 14, 1946, in Minneapolis. She was twenty-five. He was twenty-seven.

Virginia & Lloyd Smith on their wedding day September 1946

They moved to Glen Carbon and started a family. Stephen was born in 1947, but after two miscarriages, Mom and Dad decided not to risk another. Mom later told me that they chose adoption to make up for the babies the Lord had taken from them. First they adopted my sister, Connie, who was born in 1959. Then after Dad took an administrative position at Fort Snelling, back in Minneapolis, he and Mom decided to add one more child to their family. I was not quite two years old when I was placed with the Smiths on March 13, 1964, by Catholic Charities, having spent almost a year in foster care. My adoption was finalized April 12, 1965, a couple of months before my third birthday. Not unlike the stormy day I was born, this day went down in weather history too. The Minnesota River set a record flood stage of 35.07 feet.

Susie & Connie Smith 1964

My parents named me Susan Clare. Photos taken on the day I arrived show me dressed in pink and holding a stuffed blue bunny. My dark brown hair was cut pixie style. When I first came to live with them and would go outside to play, I never wanted to walk barefoot on the grass. I would lift my feet cautiously, taking each step gingerly. I guess I didn't like the way it felt. It makes me wonder if I didn't get outside much during the foster phase of my life.

The farthest back I can remember is when I was four, and my family drove to South Dakota to visit my mother's brother and his family. My parents took a long time planning the trip, and the ride itself seemed endless. I remember walking across a large yard on my uncle's farm to collect chicken eggs. I remember sitting around the farmhouse kitchen table and drinking my milk, which was thick and creamy. I also remember trying to climb out of my crib after being left in the dark to fall asleep. Beyond that I don't have many early childhood memories.

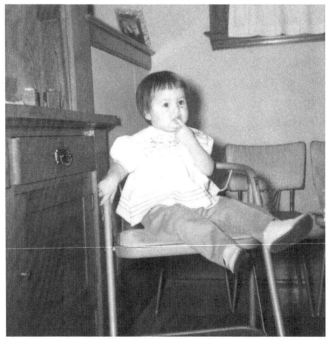

Susan Smith 1964

Many years later, my mother told me that when I came to live with her and Dad, I came with a prescription for a drug that relaxed me so I would be content to stay in my crib. It's too long ago now for my mother to remember how long I took the drug or what its side effects may have been, but back in those days, parents trusted the advice of their doctors without question. Was that drug the reason I don't remember much of my early childhood?

Other than visiting Mom's relatives in South Dakota, we didn't take many family trips when I was young because of Dad's work schedule. Occasionally, however, we took trips to cities where he had business, or we went camping. We visited most of the state parks in northern Minnesota and a few in Winnipeg, Manitoba Canada. We wore out a couple of campers, one that looked like a huge aluminum pill and one that looked like an egg on wheels. One of them always seemed to lock us out, and since I was the smallest and scrawniest, I was the one who crawled inside through an outer storage area to unlock the door. I was proclaimed the hero of the day every time I did this.

I liked camping. We battled the usual Minnesota elements: rain, heat, and humidity, not to mention mosquitoes. But we'd also roast s'mores on tree twigs and swim in the lakes. I'm not sure if it was early in the summer or if the lakes were especially deep, but my lips turned blue and my teeth chattered every time we went swimming. It used to drive everyone nuts listening to my teeth chatter. I also liked meeting other people my age. It was always easy for me to make friends.

I remember one vacation I'd rather forget. I was about six years old, and we were camping near Alexandria, Minnesota, at a fishing resort. Mom and I had seen a sale sign on some wrought iron lawn furniture at a house a few miles down the road. The woman who was selling the furniture had just returned from the grocery store, and she told us to open the fence gate and head around the side of the house to meet her. When Mom closed the gate, two ferocious dogs— Dobermans or maybe German shepherds—came racing around the side of the house, growling and with teeth bared. She slammed the

Susie and Connie Elliot Avenue, Minneapolis 1968

gate shut to keep the dogs away from me, while I watched in horror as they attacked her. She withered into a fetal position with the dogs pouncing on her until the homeowner called them off. But the damage was done. They left bite marks in her ankles, buttocks, arms, and wrists. I remember the car ride to the hospital with Mom bleeding and crying in pain. Connie and I sat in the backseat in petrified silence.

Mom's recovery took a long time. She couldn't walk because one of the dogs had chewed through her ankle bone. I remember her crawling on her hands and knees for what seemed like ages. From that horrible day forward, I have always been afraid of dogs, no matter what the size. I freeze when I see a dog running at me, even if it appears to be friendly. The memory of my mother being mauled by those two dogs still haunts me.

Our home was at the corner of 48th Street and Elliot Avenue in south Minneapolis. It wasn't far from Lake Nokomis and Minnehaha Creek. Our neighbors were hardworking, fun-loving folks. There were plenty of kids of all different ages to play with. My friends and I spent many fall afternoons raking leaves and then using those leaves as dividers for our imaginary rooms as we played house. The sidewalks on our block were uneven and cracked, probably due to the frost melting in the spring. I learned to ride my bike on those sidewalks, and there were many times I was jolted off.

The neighborhood was filled with two-story Tudor manors, each with its own character. Our house was an exact twin of the one right across the street. It had three bedrooms, a sunroom, and two bathrooms. Our entire lot was fenced off. A huge weeping willow grew in our backyard, where Mom planted the most beautiful flower garden. I recall searching for Easter eggs there, wearing a bonnet and carrying a basket filled with plastic eggs and green plastic grass.

I loved our house. I carved my initials under windowsills and on door frames. This was my home, I reasoned, so it needed my name written all over it. To this day, I could probably tour it and still find my initials here and there.

I sometimes find myself going out of my way to drive by the old place. I'm amazed at how little it seems now, dwarfed by overgrown trees. Even so, seeing that house calms me. It transports me to a time when life was free of stress, an open book of endless adventure. As a child I felt safe and happy in that place, and I thank my mother for that. She sheltered me as long as she could from the many harsh things this world has to offer.

CHAPTER **3**

School Girl / *Fashion Model*

In 1967, the year I started kindergarten, Cathee Dahmen was signed as a fashion model by the famed Ford Agency. She had been working in New York City for no more than a year.

The Ford Modeling Agency was founded by Eileen and Jerry Ford in 1946, one year after Cathee was born. In the 1960s, the roster of legendary "Ford girls" included Cheryl Tiegs, Cybill Shepherd, Cristina Ferrare, Jean Shrimpton, Lauren Hutton, Naomi Sims, Susan Blakely, Twiggy, Veruschka—and Cathee Dahmen. This was the "youthquake" era, the label that Vogue editor in chief Diana Vreeland gave to the teen-dominated cultural movement of the 1960s. Mary Quant's miniskirt, Andy Warhol's pop art, and the British music invasion captured the energy of the decade.

Models of the era had their trademark features: Hutton's gap-toothed smile, Twiggy's boyish body, Veruschka's voluptuous lips. Cathee created her wide-eyed look with spiky false eyelashes that she split with a razor. She appeared on countless fashion magazine covers, yet she had the ability to never appear the same way twice in any of her photos. Her dark brown hair and dark brown eyes gave her an exotic air. She could look like your average American girl in one shot, then Asian or Italian or Native American in the next.

My parents knew from the start that I was Native American. So, I think, did I. But when I looked at myself in the mirror, I didn't see myself as Native American. I didn't see myself as different from the kids I knew or went to school with. I simply saw myself as a white girl who tanned a little easier than some of her friends.

If anyone treated me differently, it was the nuns at my Catholic grade school. A couple of them singled me out and made me feel inferior to the other little girls in my classes.

Budding Artist

I went to several Minneapolis schools, starting with Resurrection for kindergarten through third grade. I remember competing in an art contest among third-graders in the Minneapolis and St. Paul school districts. Each pupil was to paint, color, or draw a picture to illustrate the song "March of the Toy Soldiers." I didn't think much about it or try terribly hard, although I remember being aware of the odds of winning. I just colored what I saw in my mind when I closed my eyes. I colored ballerinas dressed in pink tutus. I colored marching toy soldiers with windup keys on their backs, looking as if they were marching in a parade. I colored streamers and balloons to show the festive march.

To my surprise, I won the contest. My prize was a train trip to Duluth, Minnesota, to see my picture displayed in the Duluth Art Gallery. My mother framed it as if it were a painting by Picasso. From that point on, I knew that I really loved art. It came easy and naturally, although I had no idea how or why. No one else in the Smith family was artistic.

I have other artwork I saved from my years in Catholic elementary school. I use one of my "masterpieces" every day. It's a wooden cutting board shaped like a pig that I made in the fourth grade. I scrawled my name on the back of the board after I had cut, sanded, and varnished it. I gave the board to Grandma Rose, my mom's mother, who used it for many years. When she passed away in October 1996, I made sure that it was returned to me, and I have used it ever since.

Resurrection School always had awesome church carnivals. I remember the Octoberfest raffles and the smell of caramel apples, cotton candy, and hot apple cider in the air. But one year our family stopped going to the festivals because I was asked to leave the school. In the third grade, I got into a fight at Resurrection with another girl. She fell off the playground jungle gym and onto the asphalt blacktop and broke her arm. I didn't cause her fall, but I was blamed for it, and my parents were asked to find another school for me to attend. (My sister, Connie, being of Irish descent, remained at Resurrection until she graduated from the eighth grade and went onto Regina, a private Catholic high school.)

Looking back, I think the nuns knew that I was Native American and worried that I would become unruly and hard to manage because of my Indian blood. Why else did they favor my blond-haired, blue-eyed classmates? So in fourth and fifth grades, I was sent to St. Joan of Arc, a "free" Catholic school that was more liberal than your typical parochial school. The classes integrated all grade levels and both genders. My English class, for example, included boys and girls from grades one through seven.

Even gym class was the same. I once had to play dodgeball with a bunch of older black boys who basically ruled the school. Here I was, this little fourth-grade girl, on a dodgeball team with half a dozen sixth-grade boys. The meanest, toughest kid in the school, Collin, pegged me as the weakest team player. By smacking me with the ball, he could send me down and out, possibly for the count. I held my breath as I anticipated him launching his best shot in my direction. I planned to duck out of the way as quickly as possible, but instead I caught the ball right in the gut. The sound of that ball smacking my stomach seemed to echo throughout the gym. So did the howls of my team members, who were as amazed as I was that I caught the ball and got Collin out.

If I had one complaint about my school days, it was that my lunches were lame. I suspect that every kid who brings lunch from home hides what's been packed. I hid mine for the way they looked. When my mother finished making my peanut butter sandwiches, she used to swipe the knife on the outside of the bread and then stuff the sandwiches into Baggies. I got teased about that skid mark on my sandwiches. Seems the kids were always laughing at me at our lunch table.

By 1971, when I was in the fourth grade, Cathee regularly appeared in Harper's Bazaar *but also* Vogue, Glamour, British Vogue, *and* French Elle. *She modeled haute couture and ready-to-wear. She was as recognizable as Twiggy on the world stage of fashion modeling, becoming even more famous perhaps than her uncle, artist George Morrison. Cathee was paid well for her work and by the late 1960s was making millions of dollars, becoming one of Eileen Ford's top earners. Cathee's life was fast paced as she jetted around the world for photo shoots and glamorous parties with rock stars like Mick Jagger and fellow model Jerry Hall. Photographer Bill Cunningham remembered that during this time Cathee shared a tiny apartment in New York with a French fellow she met while modeling in Paris.*

Cathee Dahmen by Helmut Newton for Elle Magazine 1968

Cathee Dahmen photographed by Neal Barr 1968

My Parents' Dream Home

It was around 1972 that my parents found their dream retirement house. It was a rundown fishing resort in Northome, Minnesota, called Danola Lodge. It was just outside the western border of Chippewa National Forest, 240 miles due north of the Twin Cities and forty miles northeast of Bemidji. Established circa 1914 by Leola and

Daniel Thompson, Danola Lodge was a handsome and popular get-away for anglers in the 1920s and 1930s. Perched on the north shore of Island Lake, which, in fact, does have an island in it, the lodge had five stone fireplaces and a rock foundation under the entire place. At suppertime the resort cook would ring a bell that could be heard around the lake, alerting fisherman to come in for a home-cooked meal. The lodge had been neglected for many years by the time Mom and Dad bought it, but they saw in it a beauty that would take them years to reveal. For sixteen years it was their ongoing weekend project to remodel and restore.

To this day Northome (population 200) doesn't offer much more than gravel roads that kick up dust, running creeks that are filled with minnows, and June bugs that glow at night. Its main street is only one block long. It's a place where young people can break some rules, but mostly it's filled with genuine folks: old-timers who worked twelve hours every day of their adult lives, churchgoing people, women who attend birthday clubs, men who belong to the American Legion. Men gather at the local gas station to drink coffee in the morning and yak about fishing or hunting before heading out to do their work—usually farming, milling, or logging. My parents fit right in, although it took almost ten years for the residents to consider them part of their town. Until then they were city folk.

It was a lonely place for a young kid, and at first I didn't want much to do with being there. With all the lodge renovations going on, there was little time for fun. Sure I could swim, but there was nobody to swim with. I was bored out of my mind because nobody would take me fishing or boating. I had to keep myself happy. I tried to make my own kind of Dr. Scholl's shoes out of the leftover construction wood, as well as a slide down to the lake for Dad's minnows. It was always hot and buggy. Mom made Connie and me pick berries so she could make jellies and jams, but I'd rather be coloring or drawing.

But because of their love for it, eventually I fell in love with it too.

Mischievous Kid

Like most kids, I raised a little Cain from time to time. Once when I was eleven or so, I got into trouble while my parents were up north for the weekend. They hired a nanny, Martha, to watch me and my sister. Martha was mean and old, and I was afraid of her.

The trouble started when a friend told me she was making a ton of money by taking Coke bottles from the return area at the entrance of a store, sneaking past the butcher counter, and getting in line to "return" them for a few pennies per bottle. It was a pretty slick scam, and it worked—until I got grabbed by the butcher, that is. He stood there in his bloody apron and yelled at me, demanding that I tell him my home phone number so he could call my mother. I began crying. All I could think about was how much trouble I was in and that the only person at home was Martha. So I called my friend Tara, whose mom (Sally Skahen) I knew would be kinder than the nanny. When Tara's mom answered, I began talking to her as if I were her daughter. She knew who I was, but I was pretty sure she didn't know why I was calling her "Mom" until I broke the news about being caught shoplifting.

Tara's mom came to my rescue, then chewed me out all the way home about letting her down, and about how my mom and dad were going to hear about this. But she didn't tell Martha. I'm sure she figured that getting reamed out once that day was enough. I was so ashamed of my crime that I didn't go back to that store for months. When I finally did, I noticed that the pop bottle return area had been moved away from the front of the store.

I nearly got into trouble one fall day for trashing leaf bags that neighbors had worked all day to fill. My friends and I made sure we picked on neighbors a few blocks away from us. After we destroyed several bags that had been neatly filled, tied, and piled in the front yard of one house, the owner actually got into his car and chased us several blocks in his vehicle. My heart pounded as I raced home, hoping I could dive in the front door and slam it shut without letting on to my folks what trouble I was in. The last thing I wanted was a confrontation between this guy and my parents! Thankfully I threw the guy off course and made it home. I sat with my back against my bedroom wall, breathing heavily, then peeked out my window every so often to watch him drive up and down my street and in and out of my alley. I can still see his jugular veins sticking out of his neck as he yelled at me and my friends.

Junior High

I spent seventh and eighth grades at Annunciation, a Catholic school in Minneapolis. More often than not, Mom would help me with homework projects, and we loved working together. Our papier mache' models of Paul Bunyan and Babe the Blue Ox won first place in one school contest, and the principal displayed our rendition of these Minnesota folklore characters in a glass case in the school foyer.

Then there was the assignment in my social writing class that asked for a report on discovery or being free. I decided to buck the instructions and brought in my 45 rpm record of "I Can See Clearly Now" sung by Johnny Nash. I used colored pencils and crayons to create about twenty-five sketches to illustrate the song. While the song played, I displayed my sketches to the class. Some of the kids thought it was cool, while others rolled their eyes as if to say, *What an easy project for her!* Because my friend Cathy had forgotten her assignment at home, I added her name to mine at the last minute and let her flip the sketches in time to the music. The teacher gave me an A for creativity and gave Cathy a C. To make matters worse, she told the class that Cathy could not *possibly* have had anything to do with the project because she wasn't as artistically talented as I was. Cathy was relieved that she got a passing grade, but she was humiliated in front of the class. It was a good life lesson for both of us, I guess: you can't fool people by passing things off as your own when they aren't.

My social life was typical for the age. I was invited to Saturday night sleepovers and birthday parties, most of which consisted of eating pizza delivered from Beek's and going roller-skating at the St. Louis Park Roller Gardens. Anybody who was anybody went to the Roller Gardens. Dressed like sweet and innocent pro roller skaters, my girl-friends and I turned the head of every thirteen- and fourteen-year-old boy (sometimes fifteen- and sixteen-year-olds too!). I usually wore a soft-pink peasant shirt, tight jeans, and white leather skates with pow-der-pink pom-poms. You weren't shit unless you were skating backward to Barry White's "I Can't Get Enough of Your Love," index-finger danc-ing in the air. We lived for "snow balls," in which the boys skated up to the girls for a slow skate under the disco ball in the dark.

Susie backyard of 48th & Elliot Minneapolis, MN

My girlfriends and I were totally boy crazy. My first kiss was with Jim Bussen, a red-headed classmate at Annunciation who was the son of a dentist. We were in eighth grade at the time. We kissed on the playground of Pearl Park not far from where he lived. We parted ways in ninth grade when I went to Ramsey Junior High School in Minneapolis and Jim attended a Catholic boys high school in Minneapolis. Some years later I received a Valentine's Day card from Jim. He sent it to my mom and dad's house on Elliot Avenue, not realizing that I was already married. I was touched that after all those years, he would take the time to write me a Valentine. We are still friends to this day.

Ramsey Junior High

There's only one way to describe what it felt like to go to a public school after eight years of parochial education: I was free! No more daily religious instruction, no uniforms, no more scowling nuns. I liked the diversity of it all, not to mention the better boy-to-girl ratio.

Susan Smith Grade 9 –Minneapolis Ramsey Junior High

I met my first boyfriend, Patrick Berg, the summer before I entered ninth grade. We had a new kid named Steve L. who just moved to the neighborhood. Steve was rumored to be really cute. I decided to get serious about walking my dog, Nicky, so I could accidentally on purpose run into him. One day I rounded the corner at the end of my block to find Steve & Patrick Berg working on a Pat's mini-bike. As I walked by, I got whistled at, but I couldn't tell if it was Patrick or the new kid. I wasn't sure what to do, so I kept walking. Eventually Patrick caught up with me, and long story short, he became the perfect first boyfriend, the kind every girl dreams of. Pat and I entered 9th grade public school together. It was a relief to start a new school already in a steady relationship. Our ninth-grade classmates voted us "cutest couple" in the yearbook. Pat and I were serious for at least a year. But when he started smoking pot, he turned into someone other than the sweet boy I had first known. He just hung out with other potheads and began lying about where he was and what he was doing. I broke up with him, even went out with distant friends of his, yet somehow we remained friends. I could always talk with Patrick when I needed a friend.

Susie Smith & Steve Smith (brother) 48th & Elliot Minneapolis, MN 1976

High School

The fall of 1977 was memorable for two reasons. First, my high school, Minneapolis Washburn, won the regional state football champion-ship. I was on the drill team for the marching band, which performed at almost every game. Second, I got asked out by a senior!

Susan Smith Minneapolis Washburn Class of 1980

Greg Reimer and I met at a Friday night school dance mixer. He drove me home, walked me to the door, and gave me a good-night kiss. I asked him if he wanted my phone number, but he said no; he'd look me up and call me over the weekend. This guy was actually going to look through all the Smiths in the phone book for the one on Elliot Avenue? I was impressed! I waited all weekend for him to call but never heard from him. Come Monday I tried to avoid him at school, but he finally caught up with me and confessed he had looked for my phone number all weekend. When I acknowledged that trying to find it would be like finding a needle in a haystack, he asked what I meant by that, because there weren't that many people named "Paper" listed in the white pages. Turns out that he saw "Paper" written on one of the newspaper boxes on our front steps and thought that was my last name! We dated just long enough for me to get to drive his 1973 Buick Skylark—the first one I ever drove on my own and without a license.

On Friday and Saturday nights, I'd go to the Mann France Avenue Drive-in in Bloomington with my usual dates. But it wasn't long before I began making friends with kids who used drugs. I tried pot, then I started smoking it every day. I smoked it on the car ride to school, on my lunch hour, and on the way home. Most of my high school years were spent getting high and skipping school, although I rarely skipped art. It was my favorite class. I learned so much from my art teacher, Mr. Schaurer, and had dreams of a career that had something to do with art. I wasn't sure how or why creativity came so naturally to me. I just knew that was all I really wanted to do.

I had no idea that this talent, this gift, ran through my blood.

CHAPTER 4

Party Girl / *Celebrity Wife*

In March 1971, when I was nine, Cathee married Leroy Winter, the British heartthrob. He was twenty when he and Cathee married in the Wandsworth area of London; she was twenty-five. Leroy and Cathee may have met through Vogue connections, since both had appeared on the magazine's pages in 1968, or perhaps at a celebrity party. In any event, Cathee decided to leave New York and the Ford Agency to work for Models 1, a relatively new startup firm that grew into London's premier modeling agency. She was five foot seven at that time, with bust-waist-hip measurements of 34-24-34.

In January 1972, almost ten years after she delivered me, Cathee gave birth to her second child, Sarah, in Greater London, Middlesex. In 1977, when I was in tenth grade, Cathee divorced Leroy Winter after six years of marriage.

Cathee remarried almost immediately after divorcing Leroy. She and American musician Adam Merrick were wed in 1977. Although they married and lived in London, Adam and Cathee may have met in Japan, where Cathee regularly posed for Japanese magazine covers and fashion magazine spreads. Like Leroy Winter, Adam Merrick was several years younger than Cathee.

High school was a series of parties. When word got around where the next kegger would be, everyone showed up—as many as fifty people. Most of our get-togethers were at night and outside. We had great times meeting up at different spots every weekend—someplace remote so we wouldn't get busted by the cops. My friends and I had Mississippi River parties and creek parties, where the smell of pot mingled with the smoke from our small bonfire. Our parties were always fun, even when the weather was cold or wet. We sometimes broke into singing rounds of "Black Water" by the Doobie Brothers and other songs.

During the summer of 1978, I went to Camp Quest, a nonreligious outdoor program in Tamarack, Minnesota. Several of my high school friends signed up too. The highlight was a canoe trip down the Tamarack River to the headwaters of the St. Croix in Wisconsin. The campers traveled in groups of three canoes, each with three persons. Our group tried to lag behind or get ahead so that our camp counselors wouldn't catch on that we were all stoned. Each of us had brought our own bag of weed, so we smoked up a storm as we took turns paddling and catching some rays.

One afternoon we paddled about two miles ahead of the other groups and found ourselves in the middle of a lake and somehow headed upstream instead of downstream on the Namekagon River. We decided to pull into shore to ask for directions from this group of rowdy guys, who ended up giving us barbecued burgers and chicken and beer. We thought we had it made until they got drunk and started staring at us girls and talking like they wanted to screw us. Each of us girls instantly stood by one of the guys in our group as if we were couples, but there was no reasoning with our hosts. Before we knew it, one of them pulled out a couple of guns and started shooting near our feet. We scrambled back to our canoes, somehow found the right direction, and paddled furiously to catch up with the rest of the group. I'm not sure which would have been worse: getting shot or getting into trouble with our camp counselors.

That evening I got a little quiet time with one of the guys I had been admiring in our group. I remember sitting with him underneath some railroad trestles, listening to Jackson Browne's "The Pretender" and Earth Wind and Fire's "That's the Way of the World" in the distance and thinking, *This has got to be one of the best times of my life.*

In March 1978, when I was in tenth grade, Cathee Dahmen and Adam Merrick had their first child, Lana. They were still living in London in October 1980 when their second child, a boy, was born. He was christened Adam Jr.

In 1980, the year I graduated from high school, Cathee semiretired from modeling after fourteen years in the business. She was thirty-five years old. The family moved to New York City in the 1980s, where Cathee occasionally worked as an illustration model for Saks Fifth Avenue.

Recovery

When my dad retired in 1979, he and my mom began spending entire summers at their lake place in Northome, leaving my sister and me home alone. That summer before my senior year, I was dabbling with acid and tripping on weekends. I didn't think my drug use was too out of hand, but I gave my parents a big scare every time I came home with dilated eyes as big as saucers. So about a month after I started my senior year, they entered me in an outpatient treatment program for chemical dependency at the Renaissance Treatment Center in a suburb of Minneapolis. I spent almost an entire year in treatment.

I think back now on how much I hurt my parents with my drug use and wish I could erase that part of my life. I never intended to hurt them the way I did.

The Bat House

After completing my outpatient chemical dependency program, it was almost time for me to graduate from Washburn. I was in the class of 1980. But first I moved out of my parents' house and into a huge three-story house near Lake Calhoun in south Minneapolis with some of my closest friends: Nicole Darcy, Joanne Pierson, and Kuffy Hoye. The four of us signed a nine-month lease to rent the second and third floors of the house. We went to class in the morning and then worked part-time in the afternoon. I was hired as a phone receptionist for an insurance company. I had a soft, calming voice that put people at ease.

Our place at 3100 Dupont was known as the Bat House because on weekends we slept during the day and stayed awake at night. We had fantastic parties for those nine months. Trying to keep sober or straight while living with my friends wasn't easy, and I screwed up more than once. It must have been a nightmare for my folks, who knew that I was probably still using drugs. My mom was also worried about me living on my own. But by then she had decided to let me be my own person, consequences and all. When I did go home to visit, I'd scarf down a home-cooked meal, catch up a little with my folks, and then hurry back to the Bat House.

All of us roomies would frequent Zoogie's, a punk/new wave bar in the basement of a building in the heart of downtown Minneapolis. Most of the bouncers had gone to Washburn High. They recognized us, so we easily slipped by without them carding us. We often watched performances by one of our favorite bands, the Suburbs.

One night that winter, we got the news that Bruce Springsteen was in town on his River Tour and might show up at Zoogie's, which happened to be one of his favorite Twin Cities bars. The girls and I got all dressed up and headed to Zoogie's in hopes of seeing Springsteen. Nicole and I were standing at the bar when she gave me this weird look. She motioned with her eyes to glance at the guy in the leather jacket standing alone at the end of the bar. It took her a few tries, but I finally looked. I glanced back at her and said, "What? That guy's too short for me." The Boss let out a laugh.

Nicole and I were desperate to go to his concert the following night at the St. Paul Civic Center, but we didn't have tickets. We borrowed a roommate's car, drove across town, and spent at least an hour walking around in the cold to see if we could get in. We were still circling the building when Bruce began playing his first couple of songs. We passed a couple of security guards who were taking a cigarette break. By then the freezing temperatures had got to me, because the next thing I knew I was telling Nicole to just go along with everything I was about to say and headed back to the guards. I started to cry, rambling on and on about two guys stealing our tickets, then Nicole turned on the tears. The officers admitted to seeing two suspicious guys in the area and told us to come inside. "We'll get you into the concert," they promised, and within minutes, we were escorted to two chairs that were about twenty-five rows from the stage. Once they were out of sight, Nicole and I just looked at each other and howled! We were at one of the hottest, sold-out concerts of the year, and we had just scammed our way in.

Living with my girlfriends at the Bat House was liberating. For those few months I lived without rules or regret. Maybe that's why the time seemed right to search for my birth mother.

Searching for My Birth Mother

I wrote to my adoption agency, Catholic Charities, in hopes that they could tell me about my adoption. I knew I was Native American, but I didn't know how "Native" or which tribe I belonged to. I thought if I could prove my native connection, maybe I'd qualify for a scholarship to attend the Minneapolis College of Art and Design and pursue my dream of a career in art. But MCAD wasn't a *real* college, in my parents' opinion, not like the College of St. Catherine, a private Catholic women's school in St. Paul, for example. When I got serious about college, they said, I should let them know.

I thought I'd hear from the agency within a week of mailing off my letter. Instead it took at least a month. The reply was a three-page genetic background document that described pertinent information about my adoption but without naming names. In addition to giving details about my birth mother's family, the document (reprinted below) glossed over why Cathee chose adoption as an option.

THE BIRTH MOTHER

Prior to your birth [your birth mother] was planning on adoption as she thought it would be best for you and also because she wanted to continue her education. After you were born, she received much pressure from her family to keep you, and she changed her mind and took you to live with her married sister in Minneapolis, Minnesota.

She was in the eleventh grade in school and was hoping to continue with her education. She was interested in commercial art classes and received A's and B's in school. It was indicated that she had a very good ability in art and spent much of her leisure time in this activity. In a psychological test administered to her in 1962, she scored in the good-average range of intelligence but demonstrated superior ability in creativity. (Our file indicated that she had an uncle who was a commercial artist out of state, and she had expressed an interest in going to live with him and his family).

Your birth mother was in good health at that time, although she was said to have been hospitalized at the age of ten with rheumatic fever and chorea. There was no history of chorea in the family, and this was not completely documented by the doctors. The doctors indicated any chorea she might have had was undoubtedly related to her rheumatic fever. As a result of rheumatic fever, she had a double heart murmur so never took part in strenuous exercises. She did wear glasses occasionally for nearsightedness. She was said to be allergic to penicillin shots.

THE BIRTH MOTHER'S PARENTS

Her father was about fifty-four years of age and was born and raised in Minnesota on a farm. He was of German nationality and of the Catholic religion. He was described as being five feet six inches tall and weighing about 210 pounds with a stocky build and large frame. He had dark brown hair, brown eyes, and ruddy complexion. He was a laborer but was frequently unemployed, which caused marital problems. It was indicated in our files that he had a nervous breakdown at one time but recovered from this. He also was said to have a chronic cough but otherwise was in good health. His education was grade school.

Her mother was forty-three years of age at that time and of Indian and French background, and of the Catholic religion. She was described as being five feet eight inches tall and weighed about 143 pounds with a medium bone structure. She had black hair, brown eyes, and olive complexion. She was said to have had tuberculosis when nineteen years of age and was in a sanatorium for one or two years but completely recovered from this. She also had gall bladder trouble at one time. She did wear glasses. Her education was eighth grade. She was described as an attractive woman with a quiet personality.

THE BIRTH MOTHER'S SIBLINGS
Your birth mother had seven full siblings and one half sibling, aged from nine to twenty-five years.

- *A twenty-five-year-old half sister was described as being five feet five inches tall and weighing about 130 pounds. She had dark brown hair, brown eyes, and fair complexion. She was in good health and did wear glasses. She was married at that time. (ROSE)*
- *A twenty-year-old sister was married at the time and was described as being five feet five inches tall and weighing 140 pounds. She had dark brown hair, brown eyes, and medium complexion. Her education was the eleventh grade. She was in good health. This apparently was the sister who took care of you for a while. (MARIE)*
- *A nineteen-year-old sister was described as being five feet four*

inches tall and weighing ninety-five pounds. She was married at the time. She had light brown hair, brown eyes, and fair complexion. Her education was the eleventh grade. She apparently was in good health at that time. (ELAINE)

- *A seventeen-year-old sister was described as being five feet five inches tall and weighing 110 pounds with a slim build. She had completed tenth grade before getting married. She was said to be in good health at that time. She had dark brown hair, brown eyes, and medium complexion. (DARLENE)*
- *A fifteen-year-old brother was described as being tall for his age with dark brown hair, brown eyes, and fair complexion. He was in the ninth grade at that time. He was apparently in good health. (JIM)*
- *A thirteen-year-old brother was described as being tall with dark brown hair, brown eyes, and medium complexion. It was indicated he suffered a blood clot in the brain when he was three years old, and this caused total blindness. He was in junior high school. (MIKE)*
- *An eleven-year-old sister was described as being of average size with light brown hair, brown eyes, and fair complexion. She was in grade school. She was in good health. (BARB)*
- *A nine-year-old brother was described as being of average size with light brown hair, brown eyes, and fair complexion. He was in good health. He was in grade school. (PETER)*

THE BIRTH MOTHER'S GRANDPARENTS
Her maternal grandfather died at about the age of fifty-six from a heart condition.

Her maternal grandmother was living at that time and was about sixty-one years of age.

There was no information available on the (paternal) grandparents of the birth mother.

THE BIRTH FATHER
Paternity was not established by affidavit. Your birth mother gave the following information about your birth father.

He was said to be about eighteen years of age, and he was born in Minnesota. He was said to be of average intelligence. He was described as being about five feet eight inches tall and weighing about 143 pounds and of medium build. He had black hair, brown eyes, and medium complexion. It was thought that he completed the tenth or eleventh grade in school. His whereabouts at the time were unknown, and it was thought that he probably joined the Army. It was believed that he was of at least part Indian background. It was believed that he was born on the White Earth Indian Reservation in Minnesota.

It was indicated that his birth mother died from cancer in 1962. She had completed two years of high school. It was believed that she had been married two or three times, and there were children born from each marriage.

There was no information available about the father of your birth father.

Your birth mother indicated she met your birth father through a relative and dated him for about six months. He was aware of her pregnancy but did not help her financially. She had no contacts with him during the last four months of her pregnancy.

I was furious with my birth father after reading this document. I wanted to beat the hell out of him for abandoning my birth mother during the last months of her pregnancy. I wanted him to feel ashamed of his decision to turn tail and run. He probably saw her as just a conquest to brag about to his friends. My dad was the only strong-minded man I could compare my birth father to, and the coward didn't measure up. He wasn't father material and probably never would be. My bad opinion of him would last for years.

My roommates tried to console me about what I had learned about my birth parents, and at that moment, they felt more like family than my blood relatives could. I decided not to pursue any more information about my birth family for a while. It would only make me feel worse.

After our lease at the Bat House was up, I moved into a one-bedroom apartment about a mile away, at Thirtieth and Pleasant Avenue. It was close to the low-income housing projects of south Minneapolis and unsafe. It was, however, near several shopping areas and right on a major bus line, which was perfect since I didn't have a driver's license or car. I fell asleep at night to the sounds of gunshots, screaming, and the sexual escapades of the huge black man in the apartment below.

That June I went up to my parents' cabin for a weekend. I wanted to escape the city to spend some quiet time with my mom and dad, to breathe in the north woods air. I had no idea that on this particular trip I would also meet the man I would marry.

Tim

Flash back to the summer of '79 at my parents' place in Northome: They were roofing their cabin, and the highlight of our day was driving into town to pick up groceries or a few items at the hardware store. That's where I met Jim Fedorko. Jim owned a fishing resort across Island Lake and was helping my dad with his many renovation projects. One day Jim was eager to show us his new motorcycle. Mom asked him to give me a ride. She snapped a photo of the two of us on the bike and included it in her Christmas card to the Fedorkos. They passed the photo along to their son, Tim, who was a soldier stationed in Germany. Tim was more curious about the girl than the bike and decided he'd look me up when he returned to Minnesota.

Flash forward to 1980 and the summer that Tim came home:

One Saturday afternoon he and his younger sister, Khrissy, stopped by while I was visiting my folks. Since all I'd heard about was the Fedorkos' "other" son, Tom—captain of the football team, member of the track team, actor in school plays—I assumed Tim was Tom. After the third or fourth time I called him Tom, Tim corrected me. Then right in front of my parents, he innocently asked if I wanted to go have a beer with him. My mother blurted out a big "NO, Susie is not old enough to have any alcohol!" My mom saw no harm in my going out with Tim because he lived up north and I lived in the cities, and she knew I wasn't interested in a long-distance relationship. But she and my dad had just spent thousands of dollars on my recovery treatment, and the last thing they needed was for me to be tossing back drinks on some bar stool.

James Fedorko and Susie Smith Northome Minnesota 1979

Well, Tim and I wound up at the Northome Municipal Tavern, but the bartender knew I was underage and gave us the boot. As we drove around the countryside and talked, I forgot all about Tim not being Tom. We began dating each other and ran up expensive bills talking for hours on the phone—so much for not wanting a long-distance boyfriend.

Tim had just started a construction job in Williston, North Dakota, working nine days straight. On his four days off, he would drive from Williston to Northome (480 miles) and then from Northome to Minneapolis (another 250 miles) to spend time with me. Since he and Tom worked together, they often drove down to the cities together. Tim would drop off Tom just north of St. Paul to visit with his girl-friend, Karen, who was attending Bethel College.

After several months, Tom was making the drive by himself while Tim stayed in Northome. There were times Tim could not or chose not to come down to the cities to see me. Soon we were fighting. I was angry that he wasn't visiting me more often. He was angry that I didn't understand that he was limiting his visits because of time and money.

I was tired of waiting for Tim to decide when he was going to visit me. I was also tired of expensive phone bills. We broke up, and I began to date other guys, but my heart wasn't in it. I had never known anyone like Tim. He was a strong and self-assured country boy who would make a great husband and father. I felt certain that we'd be together again someday.

I moved back home with my parents for a couple of months because my apartment had been broken into, and I felt unsafe living there on my own. I had to follow house rules again while I was there, but my folks seemed more relaxed about it. There was almost a silent understanding that since I had already lived on my own, I should know how to conduct myself. During that time I tried to follow in my father's footsteps and applied for a job with the federal government. (Mom had always encouraged me to take a typing class in high school because she knew it would come in handy someday for a good job.) I finally got called in to interview for a receptionist position with the

US Treasury Department in Edina, a suburb of Minneapolis. I began my career as a federal employee in the audit division of the IRS in 1981.

When I was introduced to my coworkers, I met several tax auditors and tax specialists, including one man whose face made my heart stop. I had seen that face before, that intense, beady-eyed stare. It was the man who had chased me as a kid after I ripped up the leaf bags in his front yard! He had no idea that I was the one who upset him on that fall day so long ago.

In 1982 I moved into a one-bedroom apartment in Richfield, a suburb of Minneapolis. I loved it! I didn't have much to furnish it, but it was mine and right on the bus line to and from work. And as luck would have it, an elderly man named Whitey was my neighbor. Every night purple lights glowed beneath Whitey's window shades. One afternoon I walked over to his apartment to bring him some mail that had been misrouted to me. Whitey invited me in, and I quickly found out why he had those purple lights glowing day and night. Whitey was growing some of the best marijuana I had ever seen. He rolled up a joint, and we torched it. I could barely walk a straight line back to my apartment.

My mother phoned me one afternoon to tell me that a surprise visitor had stopped by their place. Tim had come down from Northome and wanted to see me. Before I knew it, he was pulling into my parking lot on his motorcycle. When he knocked on my door, I was shaking and couldn't decide whether I should let him in or hide.

I let him in.

His construction job in North Dakota was done, he explained, and the next project was in Montana. But that was too far away for him. He was moving back to Minnesota. He wanted to give city life a try, and he wanted to be with me again.

I had no idea that he was walking back into my life forever.

CHAPTER 5

Love / Marriage

It's remarkable to think how many connections I might have had with my birth mother if Tim and I had known each other sooner. Not long after moving to the Twin Cities, for instance, Tim landed a job as a sign hanger for Naegele Outdoor Advertising, a billboard company. According to a couple of Dahmen relatives, one of Cathee Dahmen's uncles, probably one of her father's brothers, had also worked as a longtime sign hanger for Naegele Outdoor. He left just a few years before Tim arrived.

Tim's good friend Jon Kusler was another remarkable connection to Cathee. Jon's mother, Marie, and Tim's mom, Carol, had been best friends since their days at Columbia Heights High School. Their sons grew up like brothers. By coincidence Jon worked at a place called Alliant Tech and reported to Darlene Oakgrove, the parts inspector in the machinery area. Darlene was Cathee Dahmen's older sister. Without knowing it, Jon had worked day in and day out for years with my biological aunt.

After Tim moved in with me, he applied for several jobs right away, but he had no immediate offers. He also surprised me with a black Lab puppy. Because dogs weren't allowed in our building, we had to keep him undercover. We named him Goober because he drooled all the time. Goober chewed up almost every light cord and end table I had. My furniture wasn't the best, but with the dog around, it was trashed. We put him in a cardboard box at night so he would stay put while we were gone during the day. We needed a new box every day because Goober always chewed his way out of it.

After applying for jobs in the morning, Tim would take Goober down to Lake Nokomis for some play time. Goober often made his way over to some girl who was tanning and sniff her crotch. Tim would stop and visit with the girls to pass the time. It drove me nuts, and I hoped that he would find a job soon.

I got my driver's license during this time, thanks to my dad. He wanted to make sure that even though I relied on the bus for transportation, I knew how to drive. Tim let me use his car while he rode his bike. I remember thinking, *This is so convenient! I can just get up and drive into work! I don't have to worry about exact change or missing my bus if I'm running late.*

Eventually Tim got word that the Naegele Outdoor billboard company in Richfield was looking for a painter. When he applied for the job, they handed him a paintbrush and a picture and told him to paint the picture onto a billboard! He told them he wasn't *that* kind of painter, but it wasn't long before they hired him as a sign hanger.

We were finally a dual-income household—and just in time. Not long after Tim moved in with me, I became pregnant.

Married . . . with Child

We hadn't been careful about birth control, so I was more scared than shocked when my pregnancy test came back positive at the Teenage Medical Clinic on Chicago Avenue in Minneapolis. I was barely six weeks along.

I don't recall Tim's proposal being anything romantic. He more or less blurted out, "Well, I guess we should get married then." I could have had the same fate as my birth mother, only the father of my baby committed to me after he found out that I was pregnant.

Tim and I decided right away to move out of our apartment and look for a house—a mobile home, that is; traditional houses were too expensive, and we barely made any money. I made the down payment with money I'd received a year earlier from my Uncle Rudy, who had been married to dad's sister, Irma. I also used part of my inheritance to start making plans for a December wedding. We bought our modest rings with the understanding that someday we would buy a bigger diamond for me when we could afford it.

I was about three months pregnant when Tim and I moved into our new neighborhood just south of the Minnesota River. I was twenty years old; Tim was twenty-three. One day while driving over to visit my folks, I saw my old boyfriend, Patrick Berg, working on his Harley-Davidson in front of his house. We sat on his curb and caught up on what we had been doing since we stop dating in the tenth grade. When I broke the news that I was pregnant and getting married, it was obvious that he still loved me. "Don't marry Tim," he said. "Marry me." I was flattered that Pat still felt that way.

Tim was up in Northome for the weekend, so Pat and I went out to eat and ended up back at my apartment, where we talked until the early morning hours. We ended up falling asleep on the couch. When I woke in the morning, he was gone.

On Thanksgiving Day, November 25, 1982, a fire in downtown Minneapolis destroyed Northwestern National Bank. On the next day, city buses passing through downtown that weren't cancelled were rerouted, so I decided to catch one and take it as far as Grandma Rose's off Twenty-seventh and Colfax to join Mom and Dad there. It was quite snowy already for November, and when I got off the bus at Nicollet Avenue, I had to walk three blocks, up Grandma's alley, and over her fence as there was no gate. My mom gave me a scolding after watching me fall into Grandma's yard on my hands and knees, but I was in excellent health and not worried about complications.

Tim and I started going to Catholic premarital classes in St. Paul, and every time we went, we got into a fight. I often weighed these fights silently, wondering how I could ever go the distance with this man. Tim wasn't Catholic and would not be serious at the religion classes. I felt like everyone was looking at us, as if we would be the first to get divorced. But our wedding plans proceeded—and quickly. I didn't want to be as big as a house walking down the aisle with my father.

Susan Smith December 17th 1982 Mary Mother of the Church, Burnsville, MN

On December 17, 1982, Tim and I were married in a modest ceremony at Mary Mother of the Church in Burnsville, Minnesota. My mother wore a long, formal dress in my favorite color, purple. She looked beautiful, and so did Grandma Rose. Tim showed up with his groomsmen, behaving as if they had had a few drinks. Was he celebrating in advance? Or fortifying himself against an unknown eternity with the same woman?

When we knelt before the priest during the ceremony, I heard murmurs from the crowd behind us. Tim had neglected to wear socks that matched his gray tux, so when he kneeled, everyone could see his white athletic tube socks. Tim's best man, his younger brother Troy, got my ring stuck on his own finger before giving it to Tim to give to me. Then after the formal church reception and before the informal reception (with alcohol) at the hotel, we somehow locked our keys in the car. So there we stood, stranded in the church parking lot, while everyone else was on their way to the reception. Thankfully, one of Tim's groomsmen, Jim Kusler (Jon's older brother), and his wife, Joanne, had stayed behind to follow us to the hotel. Jim popped the lock on the passenger side with a Slim Jim and off we went.

I'm not quite sure when I realized that married life wasn't going to be picture-perfect, but that might have been the moment.

Reality Sets In

My wedding was not quite like those I'd seen on *Dallas* or *Dynasty,* but it was special all the same. It was the first year of marriage that was the real challenge. Looking back on it now, I realize how close we came to not making it. We had our ups and downs, but at times it seemed that there were too many obstacles to overcome. Most of our arguments stemmed from lack of money or Tim wanting to stay out late with his friends. I did not feel respected. I felt stuck sitting alone at home and keeping a house, especially with all of my friends in college.

But I wanted to succeed in marriage like my mother. Even my wedding ring was the same style as hers. She had stayed with the same man forever, and I figured that if she could do it, then I could too. So I tried to bend to avoid breaking, doing my best to adapt to being both a new wife and an expectant mother.

Tim and I spent many weekends driving up to Northome that winter. Sometimes he went snowmobiling, hunting, and ice fishing with his buddies. Sometimes we stayed at his mother's, just gazing at the frozen lake and the occasional snowmobile trailing a cloud of snow. I would sit in front of the window and wait for that bright headlight to emerge out of the darkness across the lake. There was nothing quite as comforting as the sound of his Polaris snowmobile skidding into its resting place for the night. When Tim came into the house, a cold chill and the scent of snowmobile fuel followed.

I once asked his brother Troy to give me a short snowmobile ride, thinking he would be careful because of my pregnancy. But he must have forgotten because he raced for the nearest plowed road and drove up on the very top of it. I grabbed his waist, trying to hang on, screaming in his ear, "Don't drive so fast!" We slid down sideways onto the dirt road and turned around to head back home. He sure felt bad that he had forgotten I was pregnant.

Then there was the first time I went ice fishing. Tim and his family took me out on Red Lake, and I remember hearing the sound of the ice cracking and pinging. It was eery, hearing and almost feeling the ice break apart underfoot. We were fishing on what had to be one of the most perfectly smooth skating surfaces I had ever seen. I lay down on the ice, and Tim and Troy took turns grabbing me and sliding me across the ice like a hockey puck. Tim's mother reminded us that this was probably not such a good idea.

Tim and I spent New Year's Eve 1982 in International Falls, Minnesota. For this special occasion, I had picked out a white- and red-striped maternity smock and red pants. I looked like a human candy cane. What mattered most, however, was that I was determined to be the best wife and mom I could be.

I had five months to go.

CHAPTER 6

Samantha / Sasha

With my due date approaching, my weight ballooned from 125 pounds to 192 pounds. I had a terrible habit of getting up in the middle of the night and pouring myself half a box of Fruit Loops, convinced that the milk was good for the baby; then I would wake up about 7:00 a.m. and finish off the box. Because the pregnancy was borderline toxic during the final trimester, my doctor advised bed rest for the last couple of weeks.

On the afternoon of Monday, May 23, after a Porterhouse steak dinner with Tim, I began to feel odd. Perhaps I had eaten too much? Later that evening I felt constipated but also as if I had to go to the bathroom every twenty minutes. I made Tim run to the store to buy me prune juice. By Tuesday morning, I had not slept or had a bowel movement. We both wondered if I was in early labor, but Tim chalked it up to my digestive system and left for work. I felt scared and alone. I called my friends who had children and my sister, Connie. They all said it was the slow stages of early labor. I was convinced that I'd begin intense labor with no one around, unable to reach the phone. When Tim got home that afternoon, I asked him to take me for a motorcycle ride around our trailer park, hoping the speed bumps might move things along. They didn't. The pains continued through the night, and I hoped Tim would stay home with me the next day. He didn't.

But he wasn't at work very long before I called and pleaded with him to come home, which he did. When I called my doctor, he suggested that I pour myself a drink and relax (true!). Tim went right to the fridge and popped open a beer for both of us. After another unsuccessful motorcycle ride, I asked Tim to bring me to Fairview Riverside Hospital in Minneapolis.

The nurse came at me like a ghoul out of some horror movie, snapping her rubber gloves. I quickly closed my legs and said, "Don't put me into labor if I'm not already in labor!" She laughed. "Don't worry, missy," she said. "In all the years I've been working here, that has never happened." As if on cue, my water broke and gushed out like a popped water balloon. I looked at Tim, who peeked out from behind his *Hot Rod* magazine to survey the scene. I remember thinking, "*This is it!*"

My labor started on Monday. I entered the hospital on Wednesday. Samantha Rose finally arrived by Caesarean section on Thursday, May 26, 1983. Our good friend Bob Lacey suggested her first name, and her middle name came from my Grandma Rose. I wanted the legacy of this wonderful person to be part of my daughter's life, even after she was gone. Only years later did I learn that "Rose" was my original middle name as well the name of my birth mother's oldest sibling.

Tim took to Sam in a way I never dreamed he would. I could not imagine the depth of his love for her. He held and cradled her as if he'd been doing it all his life. He fed and diapered her without complaint. We were a very close family. Everything was perfect for the three of us.

I had a hard time going back to work at the IRS audit division after my thirty-day maternity leave ended. Our office in Edina had closed, and we had merged with the downtown Minneapolis office. The bus ride was long and smelled like diesel exhaust. I was sensitive to odors before, during, and after my pregnancy, which I think affected Samantha too. To this day she can't tolerate the smell of diesel fuel. And being so far away from her during the day was stressing me out. I lasted about three months. If I had to find a part-time job slinging drinks, I would, just to be with Sam during the day and with Tim at night.

I began a waitressing job at Russ's Pub in Burnsville, which allowed Tim and me to take care of Sam tag-team style. He worked early in the morning and was home by 4:00 p.m. I had to be at the pub by 4:30 p.m. and usually worked until midnight. Sometimes I had an after-work cocktail with the bar staff, but I didn't do this often because it bothered Tim that I got home so late.

Tim and I took great care of Samantha, but sometimes I worried about making the right decisions for her. Did my birth mother have the same worries about me, or did she leave my care up to her older sister who babysat me? I was convinced I'd never know.

Tim, Susie & Samantha Fedorko December 1983

I remember looking into Samantha's eyes when she was about eleven months old, the age when I was given up for adoption. I wondered how anyone could ever leave behind something so precious. I broke down, thinking how terrible it must have been for my birth mother to part with me. It would rip me apart to be separated from Samantha. But how could I compare my situation with my birth mom's? I had Tim's support, both emotionally and financially. Cathee, it seemed, had neither.

Every now and then I tried to connect with the adoption agency again. Every time I called I felt certain that *someone* was looking for me. Every time I called I got the third degree: What was my current address? Who could they contact if they couldn't reach me? They seemed to require more information than they were willing to give. What I got in return was the false hope that someday I would get a call from someone looking for me. What I got instead was the message, "Please send your request in writing, and it will be replied to you in letter format."

I was always checking Sam when she napped just to make sure she was breathing. One afternoon when I put her down for her afternoon nap, her umbilical cord was just about ready to fall off. I remember freaking out when I picked her up, and it was gone. What a horrible mother I was! I had lost my daughter's belly button!

Tim had Sam convinced that she could not go to sleep at night without tapping Buck, Haas, and Sunny. Buck was the twelve-point buck that Tim had shot and mounted; they were featured in the *StarTribune* for the record catch. Haas was the twenty-five-pound northern pike that Tim landed on a 1982 camping trip in Canada. Sunny was the two-pound sunfish that Tim caught when he was a little boy. Tim's parents had Sunny mounted, and when Tim moved out of their house, so did Sunny. So every night Samantha would give each one a good-night tap with her little hand.

Not long after Samantha's second birthday I became pregnant again. This was supposed to be a happy time for me, but I was grieving. I had received word that my first boyfriend, Pat Berg, had been killed in a motorcycle accident. He was twenty-three. His death and funeral had come and gone without my knowing. I truly believe that if you don't go to funerals, you haven't had a chance to say good-bye. I've never really gotten over the fact that Pat is gone.

Since I had had Samantha by C-section, we decided I'd deliver this baby the same way. Tim, who was still working for Naegele Outdoor Advertising, suggested that I drive myself to the hospital and get checked in so he wouldn't miss out on a half day of work. That was June 18, 1985. I waited and waited for Tim to show up so we could go into the delivery room together. When the phone finally rang, it was Tim's dad, Jim, wondering if we were all ready for the new baby. I started to cry, telling him that Tim wasn't there. Jim got so mad that he and his wife, Joanne, drove there to be with me. It was their anniversary, they said, and what a present this would be!

When Tim finally arrived, I was being wheeled into surgery for my spinal block. I was not yet twenty-three, but I had decided that this baby would be my last and had signed the papers to have my tubes tied. "Wait!" Tim said when I told him. "Shouldn't we talk about this?" I told him we could have if he had shown up earlier. If he wanted more children, he'd just have to find someone else.

When the surgeon delivered the baby, Tim said excitedly, "It's a boy!" The doctor looked at him with an eyebrow lifted, pointed to the umbilical cord wrapped around the baby's leg, and said, "That's not what you think it is, Mr. Fedorko. You have a daughter."

Sasha's delivery was much different than Sam's. This time I knew I could call some shots. For one thing, I wasn't afraid to ask for drugs for the pain. Morphine worked wonders. I can see why people get addicted to it! Only a few hours after she was born, I received several phone calls from family members wanting to know the baby's status. I talked for a brief time to everyone, but my voice sounded like Minnie Mouse. I kept telling them, "Oh, she's so cute." I sounded hilarious—until Tim took the phone away from me. Around 9:00 p.m. he left the hospital to get Samantha, who had been staying with our friends, the Jensens, and take her home for bed. I called Tim about 10:45 p.m. and told him that the hospital was so great, they even had fireworks! The nurses had to reassure Tim that I wasn't going around the bend. My room overlooked a nearby park that was having a fireworks display as part of the Burnsville Fire Muster Festival. It wasn't the morphine that was making me loopy!

Samantha was the one who picked out Sasha's name. One afternoon Sam saw a Muppet character on *Sesame Street* named Natasha. She couldn't say "Natasha." She said "Shasha." Tim and I liked the domineering Russian name, and we chose "Adelene" for her middle name, after Tim's grandmother. Adelene Fedorko was a strong woman, a wonderful mother, and a fabulous cook; she even drove well into her eighties. I hoped our daughters would be cookie cutouts of their amazing great-grandmothers.

I came home from the hospital on my golden birthday. I turned twenty-three years old on June 23, 1985. Several family members were awaiting our arrival, and the thought crossed my mind that my birthday had turned into Sasha's day. Samantha was eager to see her baby sister, of course, and so were Grandpa Jim and Grandma Joanne and Grandma Gina. My mom had plans to stay for about a week to help me with the girls while I recovered.

I had attempted to nurse Samantha when she was born, but it didn't work. I had every intention to nurse Sasha. It made sense; I was going to be off work for a while, it would save money, and it was good for the baby. I gave it a try in the hospital, but by day three at home I gave up, much to my mother's relief. She could not stand listening to me cry out when Sasha latched on to me. I felt like a piece of celery that she was trying to gnaw for about forty-five minutes.

This girl had an appetite! I mixed her cereal with formula because she acted almost as if she were starving. I bought an Infa Feeder, which is a bottle with a hole in the nipple that is bigger than usual. I'd load it with an entire jar of baby food, and she'd suck it down in a minute. I pulled it out of her mouth with a popping noise, and then she'd start wailing for more, so I had a second Infa Feeder ready to go. Sometimes her tummy was so full she couldn't wiggle her torso, only her arms and legs. Tim and I used to laugh at her as she lay there like a white wood tick with her little arms and legs moving. Tim nicknamed her "Budger," and to this day we still call her that!

As Sasha grew a little older, she didn't express herself well, with either words or sentences. She pronounced her S's as D's. She didn't call Samantha by her name; it was always "dister" for "sister." Tim and I and Sam understood what Sasha said, but others couldn't unless they were around her constantly. Samantha always translated what her sister said when the girls visited their grandmothers, especially Grandma Carol. I must have encouraged Sasha to keep talking that way because it was so darn cute. I never realized I was doing that until my sister, Connie, told me to stop talking baby talk to Sasha. I tried to stop, but it was so hard.

Sam and Sasha were inseparable in their early years. They kept each other entertained, and Samantha was an excellent older sister, always looking out for Sasha. She helped Sasha learn how to walk and talk. It made me happy that they loved each other and that they were so close during these early years. It also made me wonder what I must have gone through when I was in foster care and had no sister to play with and depend on to keep me safe.

Back when I was pregnant with Sam, I was scared of becoming a mother. It's not that I didn't want to be a mom; it's just that I was unsure of myself. With Sasha, I finally felt at ease in my role as a parent.

CHAPTER 7

Hard Times / Good Times

Samantha Fedorko - Tim Fedorko - Susie Fedorko & Sasha Fedorko 1987

In the early years of our marriage, we were a struggling young family, living paycheck to paycheck in a trailer park. We didn't make much with me waitressing at the bar and Tim working at Naegele as a sign hanger. But I made sure that he did the things he wanted. In the summer he went to Northome to go fishing. In the winter he went to Northome to go snowmobiling and ice fishing.

You could almost see the change come across Tim's face when he was driving to Northome. He visibly relaxes as he leaves the city traffic and noise behind. The people who live up there are authentic, fun country types. He has friendships that go back to his early twenties. When he gets together with the good old boys in Northome, they start speaking in an accent entirely their own. It all started with a story about a local named Rhett Breeman, a fellow who wore bib overalls and bathed once a month in the lake. His accent made him sound like his name should have been Cletus. After several drinks, the fellows would take turns mimicking Rhett, making everyone in the bar laugh hysterically.

The municipal bar in Northome can be either the most crowded watering hole within twenty miles or a deserted place with only one person drinking. I have seen people from the city come up for a relaxing weekend of fishing and end up passing out in front of the municipal bar and getting eaten alive by mosquitoes. The locals barhop from town to town for excitement. Six of us once climbed into Al Ungretcht's semi (without the trailer) and went barhopping. We went to the little town of Funkley (population nine), where we drank all evening and then tried to make it back to Northome for last call. We piled into the semi and drove about one hundred miles an hour to make it back in time.

My favorite bartender in Northome is a gal named Sis. She's the sister of Tim's good friend Yogi. Sis (Sandy Nelson) has had a hard life in this town of 200, and yet there's nothing she wouldn't do to help someone out. Sis wears little to no makeup and can put a 250-pound man in his place with a choice word or two. I never saw a girl slice someone into shreds with just her words. One time when she was bartending, I saw a table of five men whine about not having their ashtray emptied. Sis strolled over, picked up the ashtray, and dumped it into the biggest guy's lap. She howled, "How's that? Now get the fuck out." Sis can make your jaw drop.

Sis was also a waitress at the town café once upon a time. While we were visiting one weekend, Tim and the girls and I stopped in to have breakfast. Always happy to see us, Sis pulled a pencil out from behind her ear, licked the lead tip, and stood ready to write. She asked us, "Good morning! How'd you like your chicken abortions this morning?" I've never had my breakfast order taken quite like that before. I just love her for who she is and will always think of her as a friend.

First Vacation

In February 1988, Tim and I took our first vacation together away from the girls. We traveled to Mazatlan, Mexico, with Donnie, a co-worker of Tim's, and Donnie's wife, Linda. Mazatlan was the only warm destination we could afford. We went over Valentine's week, which happened to be the same time that President Reagan was visiting Mexico's president. As luck would have it, Reagan was staying at our hotel, or so we were told, and when we attempted to check into our rooms, we were turned away and sent to another hotel down the coast. I was not happy with that arrangement; we ended up too far away from the night life.

Our first night in Mexico, Tim and I strolled along the Pacific Ocean. Neither of us had seen the sea before, and Tim wanted to run hand in hand and jump in. I refused. We were barefoot, it was dark, and I was worried about broken glass in the sand. "I can't believe I brought you all the way down here to Mexico, and you won't even go in the water!" he said. I sat on the beach while he went in. All of a sudden he yelped in pain and headed back to shore. Even in the darkness we could see that something had taken a big chomp out of his ankle.

Three days later, when Reagan left Mexico, we were allowed to check into our original hotel. At last our trip seemed to be back on track—until Valentine's afternoon, that is. Tim went for an afternoon stroll while I got ready for what I hoped would be a romantic evening. As it got later and later, I wasn't sure whether to be worried or mad, but by eight o'clock I decided to go to dinner by myself. When I returned to our hotel, I heard drunken voices and loud music coming from our room. I opened the door, and there was Tim with some locals he'd met up with on his stroll. They'd been drinking (obviously), and Tim had lost track of time and forgotten it was Valentine's Day. The locals did not quite understand English, but they definitely understood that I was pissed when I kicked them out. I was still pissed when Tim finally woke up the next morning. It was a memorable Valentine's for all the wrong reasons.

The Fire

Our return flight landed in the frigid Twin Cities about 11:00 p.m. Tim's brother Troy was supposed to pick us up at the airport, but he wasn't there and didn't answer when we phoned. Tim tried his dad but no luck there either. The whole thing was odd. When Donnie and Linda called for their ride home, Donnie pulled Tim aside to tell him there had been a freak fire in our mobile home. What Tim told me was less than the complete story so as not to upset me, but I thought the worst anyway. When we finally cleared customs, we saw Tim's dad and his wife, Joanne, as well as his brother Troy and his girlfriend, Karin. I saw the truth in their sympathetic eyes. I asked Joanne if anything was left. "Not much," she replied. My heart sank. All I could think about was that my suitcase of summer clothes and trinkets we had bought for the girls was all that I owned.

The Red Cross arranged for us to stay at the Red Roof Inn in Burnsville. The hotel stay allowed us to regroup before the girls came back from their stay in Northome with Tim's mother. A couple of days later, Tim and I went back with the rest of the family to see what was left of our home. Grandma Carol met us there with the girls. Samantha was 4½; Sasha was 2½. How were we going to explain to them that we would never live there again?

As we drove up to the trailer park, our home actually didn't look that bad. We saw hints of smoke damage along the trim of our roof, but otherwise it seemed okay. Of course we were seeing only the front of the house. When we went around to the back, our deck steps were charred, and when I stepped inside I could smell the awful burned carpet and paneling. I walked around my kitchen, thinking about all the birthdays we had celebrated there and all the card games we had played at the table. My yellow Trimline phone was a melted blob on the kitchen countertop. Some photos hanging on the walls survived but not the paintings I made in high school. Their empty frames hung on the walls.

I walked into the living room. The new sleeper sofa we were still paying for on credit was a frozen and discolored lump. Sunny and Haas were no longer hanging on their wooden trophy frames, but Buck was still hanging on the wall, his beautiful points blackened and his fur singed. Most of my photo albums on the shelves were spared; only the outer edges of the pictures were damaged. Gone were my hand-made, cross-stitched Christmas ornaments, my wedding dress, and the family christening gown Grandma Rose had made. Of the few things that survived were the pig cutting board I made and my mother's old wooden spoon. Mom used it to stir Kool-Aid. As a teen, I used it to stir whatever I mixed with the vodka or gin I stole out of the liquor cabinet. As a mother, I'd used it to stir juices and paddle behinds. It was stained and chipped, but that spoon was dear to my heart.

Down the hallway were the girls' rooms, where they had played and laughed and slept, unafraid of the world. Now all of the treasures and comforts that had made up their happiness were gone. I couldn't bear to look. I had seen enough.

Firefighters determined that the fire began in our bedroom, where the water heater had probably leaked long enough to rot the particle-board floor. When the heater dropped through the floor, it severed the natural gas line. When the heater kicked on, our bedroom was blown to bits, and in less than ten minutes our home was destroyed.

The mortgage was paid for however, our homeowners insurance had expired. I think we each thought the other was going to take care of getting a new policy, but homeowners insurance seemed like renter's insurance, so why bother? I knew how quickly a mobile home could go up in flames, but I never would have predicted it could happen to us.

The fire fueled emotions I'd never felt before. I felt grateful that our lives had been spared, but for the first time in my life I felt vulnerable. We had nothing. We were back to square one. Rod and Sue

Palmquist, who had lived in the trailer next to us before moving to nearby Lakeville, offered to let us stay in their basement. Our neighbors held a rummage sale and gave us the proceeds. The mobile home park and our church donated several truckloads of items. Some of these items I use to this day. They remind me that without such help it would have been very difficult to get back on our feet.

I returned to waitressing almost immediately, trying to keep my mind occupied with something other than the fire. The restaurant I worked at specialized in French cuisine, and it was busy—the waits on Friday and Saturday nights were as long as forty-five minutes—but all I needed to do was to take orders and deliver the right food to the right table. It wasn't brain surgery, but my mind just wasn't there. Neither was my heart. It was hard to be cheerful and pleasant with customers when I felt like such a wreck.

I recall asking one couple how their food was a few minutes after I brought it to their table. The woman looked at me, put her index finger on her top sirloin, and said her meat was a little well done. I looked at her and laughed. "I just lost my house to a fire," I told her. "If that's your only worry, you're doing better than me." Before they knew it, I was walking away. I couldn't have cared less if her steak was cold or burned, and they had best leave a tip! Later that evening, the owner, Doug Nelson, took me aside and asked if I could go a little easier on guests, adding that telling them about the fire was probably not such a good idea.

I also remember when the cook was cleaning up for the night and rocking out to "Burning Down the House." I stood there staring at him. "Do you have to remind me?" I asked. He quickly turned the radio down and apologized. That's when I realized I needed to move on. We had survived the worst. We were healthy. We were together. We would be fine.

A New Home

I picked up as many shifts as I could, saving every tip left on the table so we could move out of Rod and Sue's basement and into our own home again. We started searching for a house immediately. Samantha was turning five in May of 1988, and in the fall she would start kindergarten. Tim and I spent two weekends going to dozens of open houses, but it was a huge disappointment. The houses either didn't live up to their descriptions, they were priced too high, or they had better offers pending.

The last one on our list, a for-sale-by-owner home, was in Mounds View, just a short distance from Tim's father's and stepmother. The house was absolutely beautiful: one-and-a-half stories with three bedrooms on a lot that was nearly an acre. It was perfect. It was somewhat chilly and muddy that day, so we did not get to tour the entire lot, but I was already dreaming about raising our family there.

Tim, his stepmother, and I went inside and sat in the living room with Mrs. French, the homeowner's wife. We had so much in common. She and I had been pregnant at the same time with our firstborn children. Not only was her son the same age as Samantha, his name was Sam too! I started thinking about how her son had grown up in that house and would have memories of it. My girls' memories were of charred rooms and treasures. My mind drifted back to the fire, while Mrs. French described the neighborhood, the school district, and nearby babysitters. Joanne, my stepmother-in-law, noticed my distraction and explained it to the woman. Mrs. French asked if we were the couple who were on the news the other weekend. I drifted back into the conversation and said yes. Then I told her that I was very much in love with the house. I didn't have to add that I would be heartbroken if we lost the opportunity to buy it.

Although the house had just been listed that day, the homeowners already had at least two serious offers they had submitted to their lawyer. We had to sweat it out for a few days to figure out the financing and to get duplicates of documents that proved Tim's veteran status. Once we knew that we qualified for a VA loan, we called the Frenches. They told us that they had decided to sell their home to us. I am grateful to this day that they chose us. We closed in April and were ready to move in.

It took just one pickup truck and one trailer to haul what we owned to our new house. Some of the donated furniture from the rummage sale was lost along the way, including a dresser that fell apart. Its mirror shattered on the freeway, and all I could think about was that we were going to have seven years of bad luck. But I remember opening the back door, walking into the kitchen, and smelling that smell that seemed like home. Twenty-five years later you can walk into the house and still smell the same scent. Mrs. French had bought an abundance of cleaning supplies and put a big yellow chrysanthemum plant on the kitchen counter.

We still had a long way to go before we could call this place home. I had no flour or sugar or salt and pepper, let alone containers to put them into. I had no laundry detergent or laundry baskets and very few clothes to wash. We had one wooden, two-seat patio chair and one lamp that sat on the floor next to the chair in our living room. I let the girls roller-skate in the dining room every day.

Everyone adjusted well to our new home, except me. I couldn't shake the feeling that something would happen again, some major tragedy, to derail our family. I started having panic attacks. I was afraid to put the kids into the car and drive to the store for fear we'd have an accident. I kept smelling smoke in the house and would run through every room, sniffing to see if something was burning. It got so bad that I would wake up in the middle of the night, jump out of bed, and sniff my way downstairs, sure that I would find something burning. I doubted myself all the time about whether smoke was there or not. I thought I was going crazy,

One day I asked Sonya, one of my coworkers at Tequilaberry's who knew about our house fire, if she saw what I saw in the sky: a smoky orange haze that hung in the distance. With a comforting voice, she reassured me that *everyone* could see what I saw. It was the sun trying to shine through smoke caused by fires burning around Minnesota during that terribly dry summer.

I tried to show the girls that the fire wasn't that big of a deal. It was only a house that we had lost, after all, not each other. At the same time, I think I had absorbed everyone's pain and fear from the experience. I was crumbling inside and kept it from everyone. When I eventually told Tim about my fears, he told me to do what I needed to feel better. I saw a psychologist, and it was the best thing I could have done. He explained that there were at least five instances that throw lives into a tailspin: death, divorce, job loss, major move, and disaster. I had just experienced three out of the five.

I saw the psychologist a handful of times and for three to four months took the Xanax antidepressant he prescribed. Initially I gained weight and had no energy, but eventually I got over the panic attacks. In time I learned to deal with whatever life throws my way. I learned to trust my faith, my family, and my friends.

Life started feeling normal again. Soon I was stopping at garage sales and meeting our neighbors. That fall Samantha started kindergarten. Grandpa Jim stood with her at the bus stop to see her off that first day and was waiting for her when she came home. Sasha and I watched her get on and off the bus every day after that. I wanted so much for Sam's first year to be perfect! I wanted her to fit in with her classmates. It made me happy to see her enjoying kindergarten so much.

Our lives were finally settling into the typical day-in, day-out patterns of most families. We had regular dinner times, play times, and bed times. Tim and I took care of the girls tag-team style. I'd leave for the restaurant at night after he got home from Naegele at four o'clock. I had dinner ready so he could feed the girls. With Grandpa Jim and Grandma Joanne just five blocks away, Sam and Sasha got to spend many evenings with them.

One afternoon before Sam came home from school, Tim brought home the cutest black Lab puppy tucked into his jacket. When I told Sam that Daddy had bought her and her sister a dog, she didn't believe me. She thought the puppy was just a stuffed animal. To prove it, she marched over to the couch where the dog was sleeping next to me, made a fist, and slugged her. I swear Sam spent the rest of Schnook's life making up for that, but Schnook had no hard feelings.

She walked Sam to the bus stop every day and kept a watchful eye over both girls as they played in the yard. At times Schnook was like their sister, growing up with them, and at other times she watched them like a mother. The girls loved her. The Black Lab (Goober) we had a few years earlier was now living with his Mom in Northome.

Sasha started school two years later in 1990, with Grandpa Jim there to see her off to school on her first day. The girls went to Pinewood, Tim's old elementary school, then to Edgewood Middle School. They participated in fund-raisers and carnivals and science fairs. One year Sasha decided to enter Tim's deer horns as her theme. She was so proud of the mount, documenting how the horns grew and where the calcium formed. At the yearly school carnival, I did face painting. I always strayed from the typical patterns, but my line was always the longest!

I made the girls' costumes every Halloween. When they were old enough to go trick-or-treating together for the first time, I made them matching clown costumes. They looked so adorable that Tim put them in the car and drove to Ham Lake so they could ring the doorbell of their great-grandparents, Curt and Alice Doemel.

During this time, the girls made good friends with Nick Hajek, the boy down the street who was two years behind Sasha. The girls thought of Nick as their little brother and still do. He's like a son to Tim and me.

Camping

School was a big part of our lives, and so were our summer camping trips. Camping was affordable; the only extra expenses were gas for our vehicle, the nightly camping fees, and ice for the coolers. Tim always managed to find wood to split for our campfires, whose glow illuminated the girls' faces before they'd snuggle into their sleeping bags. We'd make sure they were asleep at a decent hour so we could have some time to ourselves, playing cribbage over beer and snacks. I worried that bears would attack our campsite, so we were careful not to have food in the tents. Seems I was always paranoid about something and worrying about things I shouldn't have.

We tried to travel in a different direction every summer. In 1989 we headed south to the Wisconsin Dells, then made our way up to Sault Ste. Marie and home again along the north shore of Lake Superior. One night after we left the Dells, we were camped on a lake in northern Wisconsin. Sometime in the middle of the night I got up to pee, hoping Tim would have to pee too and come with me. I was petrified of being outside in the dark by myself. Who knew what kind of wildlife could sneak up on me at any minute? I grabbed the flashlight and snuck out of the tent about fifteen feet. As I scoped out the scenery on that warm, humid night, I saw hundreds of nightcrawlers popping out of the dirt like snakes in India rising from baskets to the sound of a flute. My howls brought Tim rushing out of the tent, probably thinking I was being mauled by a wolf or sprayed by a skunk. Well, his face lit up like he hit the jackpot. He grabbed a can and started plucking the worms out of the holes for fishing.

Tim and I always seemed to turn into the Griswolds when we took trips. Something bad always happened—our house burned down or our car crapped out on us. Take our 1988 vacation to Yellowstone, for example. Tim wanted the girls to have a camping experience like the one he had when his mom and dad took their kids to Yellowstone in a school bus. So we packed up the Buick with all of our camping gear and headed west via the Badlands. As usual, we had our share of adventures. This time I decided to keep a journal. Here's the abbreviated version:

August 18: Start trip at 5:45 p.m. Stop at gas station at 6:45 p.m. to fill the tank (one-quarter full) and to let Sasha and Samantha tinkle. Gas is $1.11 per gallon. I have a coupon for five cents off per gallon. Back on the road. Destination: St. James, Minnesota, population 4,364. Dinner at Happy Chef a two-thumbs up! Pull into Adrian for the night. Nice little open campground with about one hundred sites but only five campers here tonight. Dad forgot to pay L. I hear cows mooing very early in the morning. Bacon and eggs with potatoes for breakfast.

August 19: We stop in Mitchell, South Dakota, home of the "world's largest and only corn palace." We take a few snapshots and buy the usual souvenirs—T-shirts, postcards, a corn sucker for Sasha. We buy a few more trinkets at Uncle Zeke's Indian Souvenir Shop. We fill up with gas for $1.01 per gallon. The girls and Tim feed a few prairie dogs after touring a prairie homestead.

On to Wall Drug and more souvenirs! We stay at a desolate campground. Way off in the distance we see a storm approaching. It rains and rains and rains. One side of the tent collapses. By the time Tim fixes it, the other side collapses too. He ties a rope from the tent to the picnic table and one to the car to hold it upright.

August 20: Breakfast at Wall Drug. I buy both the girls a silver ring. Sasha loses hers about twelve hours later. Sam exchanges hers for a tricolored necklace (like the one I bought myself). Travel all day to the Badlands. The canyons are steep and dangerous-looking. Someone films a commercial at one of the lookout points. Tim and I wonder about the settlers who traveled through this territory in covered wagons and what they thought about seeing Indians.

On our way to Mount Rushmore, we buy scratch-off lottery tickets at the gas station. Mine's a fifty-dollar winner. Tim and the girls tour the Reptile Gardens just outside Rapid City. They see huge turtles, snakes, alligators, many different birds and lizards. We drive to Bear City, USA, a huge wildlife refuge. We see bears, of course (including cubs and one grizzly), but we also see buffalo, coyotes, rams, timber wolves, mountain goats, skunks, and cows with their calves. At Rafter J's Ranch in Hill City, we set up camp, and the kids swim in the heated pool. Porterhouse steaks on the campfire with fried potatoes, then off to bed.

August 21: We pack up and head for Mount Rushmore. Sam squeals as we round a winding curve, "Dad, I see one of those presidents!" The kids have a great time. It's a warm day, and the weather is perfect. Back at the campsite, Tim and the girls take a horseback ride in the Black Hills. Sasha's on Buttercup, Samantha's on Winchester, and Tim's on Cisco. They really enjoy the ride and can't stop talking about it. I go into Hill City for supplies. We eat pork cutlets with cream of mushroom soup and mashed potatoes. Yum!

Sunday: Blueberry pancakes and sausage, then a very long car ride to Custer State Park, where we shop and eat lunch at the Blue Bell Resort. We go to Bedrock City and visit the Flintstones Gift Shop before we get to Crazy Horse Monument. It looks pretty cool from a distance, but it looks like it's going to be a long time before the monument is completed. Samantha buys an Indian medallion made of feathers and beads. We pick out three rocks that were chiseled from the mountain at an area where you're allowed to do that.

August 22: We make our way down Needles Highway to Jewel Cave. On our way back to Rapid City, the Buick starts acting up. We cash in that fifty-dollar lottery ticket, but luckily all the car needs is a fifteen-dollar plug. We stop at Deadwood, South Dakota, sit in places where Wild Bill Hickok supposedly sat, and gamble about twenty-five or thirty dollars. The Buick is still having problems. We arrive in Sundance, Wyoming, about 1 p.m. and walk all the way to the base of Devil's Tower—an awesome sight.

We spend the night at the Days Inn in Gillette, Wyoming. A hot shower for all of us, television, and real beds!

August 23: On our way to Worland, the car is overheating. We stop and fill the radiator every hour with water from fast-food restaurants and thermoses, but it's always steaming. I step into a small army of ants that get pissed off and climb up my legs. It's hot, and I'm trying not to spill the water while I make my way back to the Buick. Tim is frustrated. We need to get this vehicle fixed in a hurry! At Cody, Wyoming, Tim pulls into a car garage. He's the only one who figures out that the car is overheating because the fan is stuck.

We finally make it to Pahaska, Wyoming, around 8 p.m. We stop at McDonald's so the kids can eat something for dinner. Tim is determined to get us to Yellowstone tonight. We fill up with gas and make our way to the east entrance. There's a "Lodging Full" sign posted at the gate, which is closed for the night. Argh! I feel like the Griswolds reaching Wally World! We set up camp in the dark at Shoshone

National Park about two miles back, at a nice spot alongside a creek. We're tired and three hundred dollars poorer because of the stupid Buick.

Next morning after eggs and bacon, we get into Yellowstone and start driving to Grant Village. The first campsite (403K) is awful. The next one (375K) is a happy medium for all of us, so we set up camp and head for West Thumb Geyser basin to see the bubbly hot pots. The kids feed a raven perched on the roof of the car. I notice elk as we drive by the woods at fifty miles an hour. Tim stops the car, and as he and I argue about whether I really saw the elk, Samantha gets out, runs into the woods, finds the elk lying like a dog on a rug, snaps a couple of photos, and returns to the car, saying, "We can go now. I got some pictures." Tim and I just look at each other.

Yellowstone is beautiful but stinky. It smells like rotten eggs. We wait a while for the geyser's next blow. Sam and Tim watch it up close; Sasha and I catch only the tail end because we are off getting her a hot chocolate. We come all this way and I barely get to witness this famous geyser blow its lid! We make our way to the Old Faithful Inn, a beautiful lodge, then go to see the Grotto Geyser. I'm not up for an adventurous hike, so Sam and I watch Old Faithful blow from the lodge window. Sasha and Tim follow the Morning Glory Trail along boardwalks posted with danger signs that show a cartoon man being tossed into the air after being gored by a buffalo. When they return, Sasha gleefully tells me, "Mom! Me and Dad had to run and jump out of the way or we would've got trampled!"

On the way back to our campsite, we see almost fifty buffalo in a herd. Yellowstone Lake is right next to our campsite, and the temperature seems the same as Lake Superior: freezing! The girls don't get in very far before both come running back with teeth chattering.

Work

In 1993 I was working two part-time jobs, one as a waitress for Tequilaberry's and the other in the fine jewelry department at Montgomery Ward. Now that the girls were finally old enough to stay at home alone after school (at least until Tim got there), I started looking for a full-time position.

Within half an hour of interviewing at a temp agency, I was hired as a staffing coordinator at its Spring Lake Park location. I liked matching people to light industrial or clerical temp jobs and working with businesses in the area. I used to joke with my coworkers that we were the best at providing a temporary ass, regardless of what was required.

Working at the temp service was like living a soap opera twenty-four/seven (we hired for all three shifts). I could write a book about the people I met. I learned about different cultures and why folks tick the way they do. I learned about worker's compensation and how some people pretend to be hurt to make easy money. I saw people who were desperate to find work lose new jobs within days because of the demons that possessed them. I watched people get off work, visit the bar a couple of doors down, and within a few hours come back to try to persuade me to close up shop and sit all night drinking myself into a stupor with them.

I quickly moved into a management position at the temp service, but I quit. I was too stressed out. I never realized just how many people would accept a job and then not show up for their shift. It was tough finding jobs for folks like that. I also found myself being stalked by a couple of male temporary employees. One kept showing up "coincidentally" at the grocery store, the gas station, the shopping mall, even once when I had a flat tire. It creeped me out.

In 1996, after a night course in basic Microsoft Word at the University of Minnesota, I applied for a job as a receptionist for a Honeywell distributor close to home. That day, January 17, we had a terrible ice storm that knocked out the power for three days, my interview being on the third day. I hadn't showered or washed my hair, but I was determined to keep the appointment. The interviewer said she hired me because she figured that anyone with that kind of desire to work would be an excellent employee. The owner loved the way I handled the phones, and he received compliments on my gentle and professional phone mannerisms.

I worked at J & W Instruments for almost two years and left only because I wanted to get back to work for the federal government. "It's a good living with excellent benefits," my dad would say. In 1998 I started working for the federal government in downtown Minneapolis. Since 2007 I've worked in the downtown St. Paul office in several areas, including benefits, staffing, and procurement. I've enjoyed it, even when I had to go on emergency details for several weeks concerning viral pig disease in Iowa and the Mexican fruit fly in California.

> *By 1985, the year Cathee turned forty, she and Adam Merrick finalized their divorce. In 1987 Antonio Lopez, the fashion illustrator who discovered her, died of AIDS. His partner, Juan Ramos, died eight years later. Family lore claims that Cathee ran the 1989/1990 New York Marathon, but the race results don't mention her, not as a Dahmen. Cathee moved to Stamford, Connecticut, where she became a computer secretary at an investment firm. In December 1996, she moved back to her home state. On Tuesday, November 25, 1997, Catherine Dahmen died of emphysema in Princeton, Minnesota. She was fifty-two years old. Her memorial service was held on November 28. She is buried in the Native American Cemetery near Grand Portage, Minnesota.*

> *Years after I was located, I came across a ticket stub for a Rolling Stones concert I'd gone to at the Metrodome in Minneapolis. The date on the stub looked strangely familiar. It was November 25, 1997. Here I was, watching Mick Jagger—someone my birth mother had known—perform on stage while Cathee lay dying just fifty miles away.*

An Easier Life

As the years have passed, our family has become more financially secure. One of Tim's dreams was to buy a Harley-Davidson motorcycle. In early April 2002, I located just the right bike on the Internet. All he needed to do was to tweak the chrome a bit and upgrade some parts. We traveled to Ames, Iowa, to buy it.

We then made plans to take the Harley for a fall color ride along the north shore of Lake Superior. Our friends Yogi and Greta Nelson joined us; so did Jon Kusler and his girlfriend. The weather was beautiful that weekend. We stopped for the night at the Black Bear Casino, just south of Duluth. We gambled and drank until early morning, then got up to continue our ride along Highway 61 to Grand Marais.

After a nice dinner, we checked into our bed-and-breakfast, which had a gorgeous view of the lake. There was a quaint library and sitting room, along with a desk that wrapped around the lakeside. We sat and drank beer on the deck. Jon and his girlfriend were in the mood to try their luck at a casino in Grand Portage, about thirty miles north of Grand Marais. I considered the ride for a moment because I have always wanted to see the "witch tree" in Grand Portage. I have always had a pull toward the tree for some reason. My butt was sore from riding all day, so I was happy to sit and enjoy the view. Truth is, I wasn't crazy about riding in the dark for fear of hitting a deer or moose. We met up with Jon and his girlfriend over breakfast the next morning. He had had such good luck at the casino that the security guards suggested that they had better be on their way.

We shopped around the bakeries and boutiques and took photos along the beautiful shoreline. The town was quiet and peaceful and seemed so comfortable; it looked like a fisherman's town but also a place filled with art and culture. I had no idea that this town was about to become more to me than just a fond vacation memory. In just a couple of months, I would find out why Tim and I should have gone with Jon and his girlfriend to Grand Portage that night.

Answers

CHAPTER 8

The Call (Part 2)

When Sarah phoned me the second time on November 25, 2002, I took the call in my bedroom. I wanted to be alone so nobody would interrupt me. I wanted to separate myself from my family in case I broke down, in case I found out that I was not who Sarah was looking for after all. It became the first step in isolating my family from my discoveries.

When Sarah called, our half-sister, Lana, was on the phone too. Like Sarah, Lana had known about me but wasn't sure how to find me. Both girls were certain that our birth mother had left a letter for me around the time I was adopted, and with that letter I should have been able to trace Cathee Dahmen and her family. Who else knew about this letter? Why was this the first time I was hearing of it?

I told Sarah and Lana about my three-page genetic history from the adoption agency. I practically knew it by heart, but I kept it within reach in case it would help me answer their questions more completely. I told them that the document noted that, after I was surrendered, Cathee moved out of state to live with an uncle who was an artist. They instantly recognized him as George Morrison, the renowned painter who Cathee had lived with in Rhode Island. When they told me that Cathee would have loved to pursue a career in art, I admitted that I'd had the same dream. And when Sarah revealed she was a self-employed graphic artist in New York, I finally understood where my artistic ability came from. It runs in the family.

Performing music was Lana's passion. At that time, she was working during the day as a doctor's receptionist in Stamford, Connecticut, but by night she sang in a band, having inherited Adam Merrick's vocal talents. Sarah boasted that someday Lana would be a famous singer like her dad. I could hear how proud she was of Lana. I admired that.

Sarah and Lana described our brother, Adam, as a little on the shy side and, like most young men his age, inclined to keep to himself. He was twenty-two, two years younger than Lana and eight years younger than Sarah. He didn't know I'd been found, but he knew I existed, and they were planning to tell him as soon as possible. I was curious. Did he look like me? Did Sarah and Lana? I had seen recent pictures of the girls on Sarah's website but not older ones of them with their natural, dark blond hair. Since Cathee was part Chippewa, and my birth father was full-blooded Chippewa, I was pretty sure that I was more Native American-looking than her other children.

As I told them about my older brother, Steve, and my older sister, Connie, I thought, *All my life I've been the baby of the Smith family. Now I'm the oldest of Cathee's children.*

As I listened to the girls talk about Cathee's career, I felt lost trying to grasp just how financially successful she had been. Within a few short years of my birth, she was earning a fortune. In an interview in the Minneapolis *Star and Tribune,* Cathee admitted to earning $2 million in 1969 alone. This new image of her as a fashion model, and a rich one at that, shattered my old notions of her as a poor teenager who couldn't support me.

Overall Sarah and Lana had had a happy upbringing, they said, but life with Cathee had not been easy. There were no rules, no discipline, and no structure. There was constant turmoil, ongoing fighting and bickering between the girls and Cathee. They described how irresponsible she was. Cathee made money but didn't manage it well. She had a habit of not paying the bills, for instance, so the utility companies would often shut off their service. She also wasn't very good about looking out for their well-being. It's not that she didn't care, they said. Cathee tried her best. But she just didn't know how to take control of some situations. So the girls lived with their fathers after they were divorced from Cathee. Sarah and Lana spoke highly of their dads, describing how close they were to them and how often they saw them. I began to hope I might meet them someday and hear their stories about my birth mother.

It made me wonder again about my own birth father. Did the girls know anything about Tommy Conklin? Sarah said she seemed to recall he had been a boxer once, adding that the best person I could talk to about the Dahmen family was Cathee's older sister, Elaine. It was Elaine who told Sarah who my father was.

Sarah and Lana described the Dahmen side of the family as very large, saying that we had many aunts, uncles, and cousins. I got so lost in listening to them that I found myself writing down whatever they said without fully processing it. I didn't even know how to spell Cathee's family name. Instead of D-a-h-m-e-n, I had been writing D-a-m-o-n, like the longtime Yankees outfielder. They admitted that they were never close to their mother's family—they had visited Minnesota rarely as kids because Cathee had kept them away—but Sarah and Lana recognized each one of Cathee's brothers and sisters as I read their descriptions from my genetic history.

I offered to fax the document to each of the girls. I wanted them to trust me and to have no doubts that my story was true. I felt that I needed to convince them that it was, in fact, *me* they were looking for. But by the end of our forty-five-minute conversation, it was clear that we all believed that I was the long-lost sister Sarah had been looking for. Both girls even said that my voice sounded like Cathee's. I yearned to have known her, even for a few minutes.

Before hanging up, the girls said they were happy to know that I had had a good family life with the Smiths. They said they were glad I hadn't lived through what they had with Cathee. Hearing that I was better off apart from Cathee was not what I expected or wanted to hear, and it hurt coming from them. They hadn't grown up feeling unwanted. They weren't carrying the baggage of low self-esteem. Cathee had a life with all her children after me. She left me behind.

The person they called "Mom" was my mother too, but I couldn't call her that. Was it because I hadn't been raised by Cathee and they had? Or was it because I was angry at her for living her life without me? There'd been only one person I had called Mom, and she had never let me down. I would be devastated without her. Eventually I found myself agreeing with Sarah and Lana that my childhood had, in fact, been positive. Steve and Connie and I had been nurtured by wonderful parents and raised with great values that I've passed on to my own two daughters.

I knew Sarah, Lana, and I had to say our good-byes, but I didn't want to let go. We promised to keep in touch. As soon as I hung up the phone, I began to cry. I was happy and sad at the same time, and I wasn't sure which side was winning. I felt as if I was coming out of a thick fog and recognizing more clearly who I was. I finally had answers to so many of the mysteries of my early past. But why did it hurt to hear those answers? Why did I feel I had to hide from the Smith family what I had learned? Why did I feel like I was betraying the Smiths by pursuing the answers to even more questions? The thought crossed my mind that I might never get the answers I most wanted. Could I live with that?

I had no idea at the time the severity of emotions and stresses I would experience while getting to know my birth families. I had no way of knowing how I'd be affected from that day forward. It was as if a small grass fire of changes was smoldering inside me, and I would not feel it till it raged out of control. I do know now that I am glad I was found when I was forty, not twenty. All hell might have broken loose if I had met Cathee back then. I am not a forgiving person.

Cross me once, shame on you.

Cross me twice, and screw you forever.

The Day After

I was excited when Sarah called again the following day. She sounded so sweet and sensitive. We both cried when I asked simple questions that she did not have answers for. One question was especially awkward: how to thank Cathee's brother Mike for being blind. His disability was the clue on my adoption search board post that made my profile stand out and alerted Sarah that I was a match. Since I didn't know him, I wasn't sure how he would react to my thanking him. Sarah explained that Uncle Mike was comfortable with his blindness and keenly aware of what went on around him. Once when she and Lana came home to Minnesota, they saw him giving directions to his brother Jimmy, while Jimmy was driving. Uncle Mike knew where all the stop signs were and where to make the correct turns.

Sarah said she had called our brother, Adam Jr., to let him know she had found me. She then hooked up a three-way phone conversation with him and me, just as she had with Lana. He talked a little about himself—he was in school and lived with his girlfriend—and he also talked a little about Cathee. He kept referring to her as "my mom." I got the feeling that he wasn't sure I was Cathee's daughter, and it was going to be a hard sell to convince him. I think Sarah picked up on that, so together we told him how Sarah had seen my post on the adoption search board; how she had tried to contact me through a moderator, who only had access to an e-mail address I didn't use that often; and how Sarah ended up calling me at work.

At some point I mentioned that I played computer games at home all the time. When Adam asked what kind of games, I felt a little silly telling him that I was addicted to bingo. There was a noticeable pause before he said, "Mom *loved* to play bingo. She was a bingo *freak*. She went to the casino in Connecticut all the time to play."

By the end of that phone call, I think Adam was more convinced than not that I was the girl he and Sarah and Lana had known as Cricket. But I realized it was going to take time to convince others of the same thing.

Aunt Elaine

Elaine Dahmen Colbert—Cathee's sister—was to call me next, thanks to Sarah's efforts to connect us. Since the death of their mother, Mary Morrison Dahmen, Elaine had been a pillar of the family. Sarah and

Lana hadn't seen Mary that often, but she doted on them when they did. She was a *wonderful* grandmother, they said. If, in fact, she had been the one who banished me from my birth family without Cathee's knowledge, then she wasn't fit to be called grandmother in my book.

I got home from work a little later than expected that Wednesday, November 26, so when Elaine called, my oldest daughter, Samantha, answered. Elaine was so happy to talk to Samantha that she started to cry, which was probably the worst thing she could have done. Samantha is ultrasensitive, and it upset her to hear a stranger break down like that. She wasn't sure how to react.

That's when I knew I was being selfish. How could I think I would be the only one affected by this reunion? On the one hand, I wanted to protect Samantha from pain, but on the other hand, I knew that she was nineteen, a grown woman, and no matter what pain she was feeling, I wanted her to try to imagine being in my shoes.

Sasha Fedorko Mounds View Irondale Class of 2003

Samantha Fedorko Mounds View Irondale Class of 2001

When Elaine called back a while later, she told me that I had never been forgotten over the years, that the Dahmen family always remembered Cricket in their conversations. She told me that Cathee was certain that I was dead; she thought for sure that I would have found her and her family from "the letter." (I never have discovered what happened to this letter.) Elaine described all of my aunts and uncles one by one, including Marie and Darlene, who had passed away. It was hard enough to keep up with their names, let alone everyone's story. Each of Cathee's siblings had a large family and, it seemed, multiple marriages. Uncle Mike was the only one who did not have children.

Elaine was afraid that I was going to pass judgment on the family, which she described as being close, despite everyone's struggles with poverty and addiction and divorce. She was afraid that I would judge her, in particular, for marrying her sister Marie's husband after her sister passed away. My head was spinning. *Married her dead sister's husband? Where the hell was my notepad? I should be writing all this stuff down!*

Elaine was excited about meeting me, and so were her kids. She chuckled because they were already hounding her about whether Cricket was coming tomorrow for Thanksgiving dinner. Perhaps we could get together over the long weekend? I agreed to make it work. I'd waited a lifetime for this to happen, and I wasn't going to let anything get in the way.

But when I tried to imagine Tim and the girls sitting down with Elaine's family, I thought, *It's too much too soon.* I could tell from Sam's reaction to Elaine's first call that any meetings between the families had to be carefully planned. Grafting my family with the Dahmens would take time and had to be done sensitively. I wondered whether I would fit in with the Dahmens. I was raised so differently. Being the baby of the Smith family, I was used to getting my way, having my parents bend for me. In the large Dahmen family, I'd be just another kid.

A couple of days after I spoke with Elaine, I received a letter from her. She didn't own a computer and didn't have e-mail. Letters sent by snail mail were her way of keeping in touch with everyone. This first letter told me as much as she could about Cathee:

Dahmen family reunion 1983 bottom row: Darlene/Leo Dahmen/Cathee/Elaine
Middle row: Rose/Marie/Mary (Morrison-Dahmen)/Mike
Top row: Barb/Jim/Peter

Dear Susan,

Before we, or I should say, you get to know any of us, I want to write down everything about our family, then let you decide if you really want to get to know any of us. There were nine of us kids, and we grew up very poor. My father, Leo, couldn't read or write, and Mom was a full-blooded Native American. We were mostly raised around our father's family, who were Germans. None of them really cared about us but tolerated us because my dad was like a handyman for his family. I'm sure they loved us, but they were very strict as far as us kids were concerned. Most of us were born around the Onamia, Minnesota, area.

There is Rose, the oldest, who now lives in Cement, Oklahoma. Marie was next; she's the one who took care of you. She died in 1986 at the age of forty-five years. Darlene, who died in 1998, lived in Brooklyn Park, Minnesota. Her husband and some of her kids still live there. Then comes me, Elaine. I live in Princeton, Minnesota. I'm fifty-eight years old and a year younger than Darlene. Your birth mother was next; she died in 1997—fifty-two years old—and six months before Darlene passed away. Brother Jim comes next; he lives in Brooklyn Park, Minnesota, and he is fifty-six years old and has a wife and four grown children. Mike is next. He's the blind one and lives in south Minneapolis with his wife, who is much older than him. He is fifty-four years old. Barbara is next; she lives in Grand Portage, Minnesota. It's the reservation where all of us kids are enrolled. She is fifty-two years old. Pete lives in Alaska; he's the baby. He's fifty years old.

None of us have very stable lives, except maybe brother Jim. We are all foolish; we all like to gamble, like to have a few drinks. Although none [of us] are alcoholics, we like to have fun. And we are just plain nuts. We do get together every once in a while. When Mom (Mary Dahmen) was alive, she kept us all real close. Now it seems like we're all drifting apart. I guess I never realized how much a mother really meant until after she left us.

Anyway, about your birth mother . . . she was always sick when we were kids, always had a runny nose year-round. She and I fought like cats and dogs, she being the cat and always with long fingernails. I chewed mine so I always walked around with a scratched-up face. We were dreamers—we were going to grow up and be somebody. She was never going to have kids and be poor like we were.

By the time we grew up, or I should say [were] teenagers, we all had kids out of wedlock. So when Cathee got pregnant, she said no way was she going to get stuck taking care of kids. Early on, before you were born, she decided to put you up for adoption. Of course we all knew she couldn't go through with it, and sure enough, she brought you home.

As I remember, Marie took you while Cathee went to finish high school. Marie was going to have a baby, and I had Cindy, who was born in February of 1962. We all promised to help. Marie took care of you for a while. I was wrapped up in my two kids and really don't know what happened, or why they took you from Marie.

Cathee always blamed my dad. Why, I don't know and probably won't ever know, since everyone is gone that was involved. Anyhow, your mother went to Rhode Island to stay with Mom's brother, Uncle George. She finished school there and went to New York, where she began her modeling career. She was on the cover of every fashion magazine for a few years. She was very famous for a while but never seemed to be happy. She married Leroy Winter—he was a movie star, mostly in England. (He starred in a 1968- Shakespeare movie; they show that movie in school—my granddaughters have all seen it.) They had Sarah. I don't know how old Sarah was when they divorced.

Soon after her divorce, Cathee married Adam Merrick. They had Lana and Adam Jr. and moved back to the United States. Cathee did a few modeling jobs and went to night school and got a job. She sent Sarah to live with her father, and Lana and Adam Jr. to live with their father, and she moved to Connecticut alone. I can't remember when it was, maybe in 1989 or 1990, [but] she ran the New York Marathon. When she finished, her lungs collapsed. That's when she first learned she had COPD, or emphysema.

She came home more often after that. Then in 1996 she came home for good. She got here on December 23. About 11 p.m. on Christmas Eve, she wound up in the hospital on a respirator in the intensive care unit for a month. She went to a nursing home after that for a few weeks, then went to stay at Mom's in Minneapolis (I live fifty miles north).

She and Mom were constantly arguing about everything. We all decided to go on vacation, so me, Mom, Cathee, and Darlene all rented a car and drove to Oklahoma, then to Arizona. Cathee was miserable the whole time, and sure enough, she wound up back in the hospital for a month. After that she came to live with me in Princeton, Minnesota.

She told me then she didn't have long to live. She was very sick most of the time, but when she wasn't, we had long talks and went to the casinos. It was there in the casinos she became a different person. It was like she wasn't even sick. We had so much fun and always won enough to stay for a while. But she always paid for it when we got home.

We talked about you often. She said she tried to find you once but guessed you weren't ready. She wanted to be a grandma before she died; she always said she probably was. She was very, very sad before she died but very brave. She didn't want to be put on the respirator again, because the doctor said she would have to go into a nursing home for good after that because her body couldn't take it.

So when she got sick and the antibiotics didn't work, she asked for the morphine drip. Before they started it, we talked for about a half an hour. She told me she was sorry about giving you away. She said how much she loved all of us, and I should tell everyone she wasn't afraid and said nobody should be sad.

She lived her life the way she wanted and accomplished everything she set out to. She made my outlook on life very different. I feel very proud to have had her for a sister. She was cremated and buried in Grand Marais. I kept her ashes for a year and would have kept them forever if it wasn't for my mother. She was Catholic and didn't believe in anything like that. So we buried her. My mom is right next to her, as I will be someday.

All of us have stories to tell, so if you really want to get to know any of us, be prepared to be surprised. I hope you've had a good life, and please tell me you did because I couldn't bear it if you didn't. I will tell you why someday.

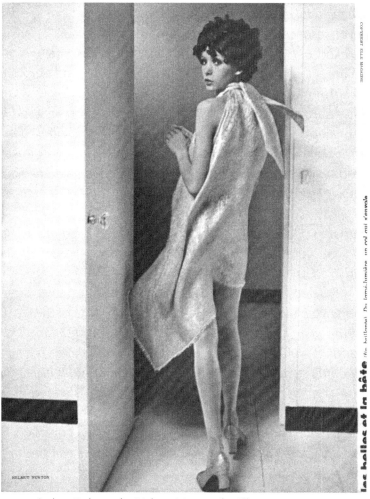

Cathee Dahmen by Helmut Newton for Elle magazine 1968

Elaine never did tell me why.

The following day I received a second letter from Elaine in response to a photo of myself that I sent to one of her friends who had e-mail:

Hi Susan,

Just got back from my friend's house with your picture. You look like me a lot, not now but when I was your age. I can see all of us in you, especially me and Tam, Darlene's daughter.
I picked out a few pictures of some of us. As you will notice, we are all very much Native Americans as [are] all our children, except Jim's and Cathee's families. Hope this is okay with you. Sister Barbara is already talking about getting you enrolled in our reservation. Has she e-mailed you yet? All the whole family is driving me nuts, calling four, five times a day. Everyone is so excited. Steve, my son, thought you were coming for Thanksgiving dinner. I tried to tell him it would probably take time.

Barbara's kids want to know when you're coming to Grand Portage. But that's our kids. All of them always knew about you, and like I say, we are all foolish.

I hope you had a nice Thanksgiving. We all had a lot to give thanks for this year: you! I wanted to call you, but with all my kids and grandkids running around, the phone ringing, and [having had] very little sleep, it was like I was floating around. If ever I wished for a computer, it's right now. I'm sort of old-fashioned though. I would rather write letters than talk on the phone or use a computer. Hope you don't mind. I love writing when I'm alone. I hope I'm not scaring you away with all my stories. I will probably be writing more about all the kids. Not only mine: there are about thirty-plus cousins you have, not to mention their kids. Some are grown; some aren't. Scared yet?

Well, I have to get ready for work tonight. It's my second job.

I think you look like me, even wear your watch on the right hand. Are you left-handed? I'm not; I just like to wear it on my right arm. You're built like me too. I'm a little large in the midsection though. Better go. You can keep the pictures if you want. I have many pictures of everyone. Will send more later if you want me to. Will keep in touch. I am so happy to have found you. I love you, kiddo.

My Birth Mother's Family

That same day I got a call from another member of my birth mother's family. The caller ID displayed a northern Minnesota cell phone number, so at first I thought someone from Tim's side of the family was calling. Instead it was Steven Standing Cloud, Elaine's oldest son and one of my many Dahmen cousins.

Steven said he was traveling from the Bemidji, Minnesota, area with his son, Myles, and was getting near the city. Would it be all right with me if he stopped by to visit? Sure, I said.

Tim's reaction was disbelief. "This is so weird," he kept saying. My phone conversations with Sarah were one thing, but now the reality of my "other" family was about to walk through our door. And if this meeting worked out, we'd probably have more long-lost relatives coming out of the woodwork to see me. Tim wanted me to be sure that I was ready for it. I think he was worried that they'd all want something from me. I was also aware that the girls were freaked about what was going to happen. For now we tidied up the house, and Tim built a fire in the living room fireplace. Steven was my first face-to-face connection with my biological family, and I wanted to give a good first impression.

I was so excited and worried I could hardly concentrate. I must have changed my sweater at least four times. Then we all just sat in the living room and watched TV like a perfect family, taking turns looking out the picture window, watching for a car, waiting for the knock on the door. Steven called when he was a couple of blocks away, and I navigated him right to our driveway. Then he pulled his car into the driveway.

When Tim noticed Steven's Red Lake reservation license plates, he called out how strange it was to have a car with "Red Lake Plates" in our driveway. I ignored his comments and opened the door. When I looked at Steven, I saw a beautiful Native American man, with hair almost the same color as mine. I saw family in his eyes. I wondered if he was the type to give long hugs. He was.

Steven said he was proud to be the first of the Dahmen family to meet me. *Wait till he gets to know me,* I thought! He then introduced me to his son, Miles. We all sat in the living room and talked for a short time. I asked him about his siblings and their ages. Did these cousins of mine know about me? Had they heard that I had been found? I also asked him his age, just to know if he had been around the year I was born and living with the family. (He was.)

Steven seemed to think that I looked like our Aunt Josie, my Grandmother Mary's sister. I wanted to know what Elaine was like. And how about Cathee? When was the last time he saw her? What was her funeral like? I was sort of jealous he had spent time with Cathee—time he probably took for granted as we sometimes do when we think we have all the time in the world.

I told him that I was worried about meeting everyone, and that I was perfectly okay doing this one person at a time. It was so much easier and more personable that way. I asked him, "Will everyone accept me?" He said, "It's not a matter of acceptance. Catherine was a significant and respected family member. You are her eldest child. Therefore, you already have status among the family."

I wasn't ready for his response. He elevated my existence in the family to a level I didn't even know was possible. Before this moment, Steven could have cut me off in traffic, and I would have cussed him out, not knowing we were related. Now, with our connection established, I sensed that he was someone I could have gone to school with, had family Christmas dinners with, and grown up with.

We could have talked for hours. After we exchanged numbers

and e-mail addresses, Steven and Myles were on their way. I watched as he backed out of my driveway and drove away. Now that all the excitement of the moment had passed, Tim and the girls went about their business like it was any other night at home. But I felt a light glowing inside me that I had never felt before.

Elaine and I had agreed to meet on Saturday, December 7, 2002, at the home of Nadine and Jimmy Dahmen in Brooklyn Park, a suburb of Minneapolis. My Uncle Jimmy was Cathee's younger brother; her younger brother Mike would be there too, as would several other Dahmen family members. I spent the morning figuring out what to wear, trying on at least three outfits, and asking Sam and Sasha if I looked all right. It wasn't just nervous excitement. I was scared, afraid of rejection. I had been comfortable with my appearance until then. Now I felt self-conscious, like I was going to be judged for not being the twig my birth mother was. I was disappointed that I didn't look like I did before I had children. I had this thick middle section, which was something I couldn't hide and for years blamed on my C-sections. I finally chose a comfortable white sweater and a pair of jeans with a brown, western fringe belt.

Tim was up north that weekend, but my daughters rearranged their plans so they could go with me. How I managed to drive to Jimmy's house is beyond me. I had no idea what was going to happen, and I was worried about thrusting my girls into this situation full throttle. We rang the doorbell, and there stood Uncle Jimmy, a strikingly handsome older man who looked like the photos I'd seen of Cathee. I felt the sincerity of his embrace, almost as if it was making up for all those years I had been separated from the family. Standing next to him was a man who held a cane, and I knew this must be Uncle Mike. He gave me a hug, and so did Wanda, his wife. I met Jimmy's kids too.

Then Elaine came forward, trembling as she reached out to me. I found it difficult to see her face with all the tears welling in my eyes. I held her for a long, long time, thinking, *I am in the arms of my aunt for the first time.* It was the next best thing to holding my birth mother.

Elaine said she had something to show me and handed me an old green scrapbook that contained hundreds of clippings of Cathee from major fashion magazines—British, Japanese, American—from 1967 through the 1970s. She modeled everything from Seiko watches to Hanes pantyhose. I was more than excited to see so many photos. I was in awe. I had no idea that Cathee had achieved this level of modeling success. I could see pride in Elaine's eyes and hear it in her voice. For the first time, I felt proud of my birth mother too.

Although the pages were not acid-free, the years had been good to them. As I paged through the scrapbook, I could see myself and my daughters in Cathee's face. She was in her early twenties in most of the photos, and I wondered what she might have been thinking as she posed on this day or that, in this outfit or that. Did she ever wonder about the daughter she left behind? Or were money and fame the only things that absorbed her thoughts?

I was surprised when Elaine told me about Cathee's tattoos. I'm not sure if any were inked by someone who knew what he was doing, but most of them were done by her sisters when they were very young. Shortly after she gave birth to me, the initials "CVD" were tattooed into the web of her left hand between the thumb and index finger. The letters stood for Catherine Veronica Dahmen; Veronica was the name Cathee gave me. Other tattoos Cathee had done herself; only the men who knew her intimately knew where they were and what they said, although I do know that the words "hot stuff" were inked on her inner thighs. I wondered if photographers had to touch up her photos so the tattoos were not visible.

I closed the scrapbook and rested it on my lap. I looked down at it several times, thinking, *That's my mother in these pages. I'm not sure if this meeting is going well or not, but I want to be absolutely clear with my memory of these photos because I am not sure if this will be the last time I get to see them.* Elaine then told me she wanted me to keep the book. I was speechless. How could she give away such a treasure? Her unexpected gift brought tears to my eyes. I looked over at my girls, and they were in tears too.

Elaine and I visited for a while, just the two of us. She told me that after I was adopted out, and after Cathee moved out east to live with Uncle George and Aunt Hazel, Cathee didn't come home to Minnesota very often. Elaine didn't go into much detail on the whys. She also talked about her siblings who couldn't be there that night to meet me, like my Aunt Rosie, who livds in Oklahoma; my Uncle Pete, who lived in Alaska; and my Aunt Barb, who lived in Grand Portage, Minnesota. Elaine told me about the rendezvous and powwow held in Grand Portage in August and said she hoped that someday I'd become a part of that annual celebration.

Before the girls and I left Jimmy's, we snapped photos of me with Elaine, Jimmy, and Mike, then some with me and the girls and everyone else. How I wish I could have been a fly on the wall after we left! What had the Dahmens thought of me? I got the impression that I would have been accepted no matter what I looked like or said. They were welcoming people, regardless of whether or not I had been raised with them.

Susie and girls meet Cathee's siblings December 2002
Bottom row: Sasha & Samantha Fedorko
Top row: Jim Dahmen /Elaine Colbert/ Mike Dahmen

The girls and I were pretty quiet on the drive home. I think each of us was running the evening's conversations through our minds over and over again. I know the girls felt comfortable with everyone they had just met, but they couldn't help but struggle a bit internally, wondering if they were somehow betraying their love for my mother, their Grandma Gina. I assured them that Cathee and her family would never replace Grandma Gina. That was simply not possible.

Later that evening the girls went out, and I stayed at home. As I pored over the scrapbook, it got me thinking: I was a collector of antiques, a habit I inherited from my adoptive mother. A couple of years earlier, I even shared a booth at a local antiques shop and tried to sell my wares. I remembered that I had several issues of magazines from the late 1960s—*McCall's, Life,* and *Family Circle.* Could fashion photos of Cathee be in those magazines? I went to my bedroom closet, pulled out the magazines, and scattered here and there in the ads was Cathee's face. She had been within arm's reach all these years, and I had no clue.

I sat on my bed and cried. My passion for antiquing had brought me closer to *both* of my mothers. I began to believe that there were coincidences that connected me to Cathee that I would never be able to explain. What other reason would I have had to hold onto these magazines for so long? I simply had to accept that some things happen for a reason and that I shouldn't question them.

I called Sarah to tell her how well everything had gone that evening. She had predicted it would, and she was genuinely happy I had met Elaine, Jimmy, and Mike. Sarah was probably the only one of Cathee's other children who had tried to connect with the Dahmens back in Minnesota.

I tried to recount every detail of the meet and greet for Tim when he came home, but I found it difficult. I guess I still needed to process it. He was happy for me, but he also warned me to be cautious. He was concerned that I would be hurt in the long run.

Over the next few weeks, I talked frequently on the phone with Sarah, but also with Lana and Aunt Elaine and Uncle Mike. I also talked with my Aunt Barb, whom I met a few months later when she came down from Grand Portage to the Twin Cities on business. I recognized her instantly from the photos I'd seen of her in her younger days. We talked for at least a couple of hours. I listened to her stories of growing up with Cathee. The family had had their hard times, she admitted, and there was little money. I felt comfortable speaking my mind with Barb, certain that Cathee had done the same.

Barb also talked about the family's recipe for Hangover Soup. I'd never heard of the soup before, but I was intrigued about what it was like, so I got the recipe from her (see appendix). I admit I haven't developed a taste for it! Perhaps I just need to work with it?

I continue to talk with Uncle Mike at least weekly. Since the death of his mother, he has felt lost. He had talked with her every day, and I was sure he missed her. He seems happy to have another person in the family to talk with.

I know the feeling.

CHAPTER 9

Cathee's Children

I often go to Washington, DC, for job training, and I was scheduled to be there again in January 2003 for four days. I called Sarah to let her know about my travel plans. Since DC was just four hours from New York, she thought it would be a perfect opportunity for her and Lana to meet up with me. I would be finished with business on a Thursday and could take an extra day of leave and stay through the weekend. We decided to meet in Georgetown on Thursday, January 9.

I made reservations for Sasha too. In recent years my daughters had taken turns joining me in DC for mini vacations. They'd take in the sights while I worked during the day, then we'd spend evenings together. I had canceled Sasha's trip the previous October because the DC sniper was terrorizing the area, and there was no way I wanted her there until he was caught. I knew I had to make good on this trip, or I'd still be in the doghouse as world's worst mom. (The sniper was arrested October 24 after killing ten people.)

Sasha arrived in Georgetown that Wednesday night. I hadn't told Sarah and Lana that Sasha would be there because I wanted them to get a double surprise: a new niece along with their new sister! And as excited as I was to meet new family, I felt comforted to have one of my own with me for this event.

The next day I reached Sarah on her cell phone as she and Lana were getting closer to the city, but with rush-hour traffic they were running a tad late. I asked her to call our room before they came up. Sasha could tell that I was nervous. I kept looking at my watch. I paced and paced. I kept going into the bathroom to check myself in the mirror. What would they think of me? I'm not rich or beautiful. I was pretty when I was younger, but now I was fat and gray, just an ordinary, middle-aged Minnesota wife and mom. Surely they'd be as disappointed in me as I was.

When the phone rang, its volume startled me. Sarah and Lana were on their way up. I looked at Sasha and said, "This is it." I opened the door to two beautiful young women who introduced themselves. "You look just like Mom's sisters!" they exclaimed. Here I had thought I looked like Cathee when she was in her twenties. We gave each other big hugs, and then I introduced Sasha. They seemed elated to be instant aunts!

I brought out the scrapbook with Cathee's magazine clippings that Elaine had given me. It turned out that they had had a hand in making it, cutting and pasting all the photos in place, during their last visit to Minnesota to see Cathee before she died and to attend her memorial service. Sarah had made a second album with some of the scrapbook photos in high-resolution color, plus other photos that I'd never seen—photos of her and Lana when they were little girls and a photo of their half-brother—*our* half-brother—Adam Jr.

We all seemed a little overwhelmed, yet I felt instantly comfortable with Sarah and Lana, just as I had when meeting all the Dahmen aunts and uncles the month before. We decided to go out to dinner and chose a nearby steakhouse. Only after we looked at the menu did we realize that the place was really pricey. I had the money, but I had no intention of parting with it. Sarah and Lana looked just as shocked at the prices as I was, so I asked if they would mind if we just paid for our drinks and went somewhere more affordable. Boy, were they relieved! The waiter acted like a snob when I told him the truth. He grabbed our menus and walked away. We found a Georgetown hangout right across the street that was serving a prime rib dinner (my favorite and Sasha's) for about $12. Everyone felt so much more relaxed without having to worry about the bill. We chilled and talked for hours.

Sarah and Lana talked about life with Cathee, the good times and the hard times too, especially during the last five to ten years of her life, when the girls were finishing high school and middle school, respectively. Sometimes Cathee was around and sometimes she wasn't. When she was home, she didn't discipline her kids. When she disappeared, she left them alone for days at a time. If she hadn't paid the bills, the kids would sit there without lights or phones while Cathee was nowhere to be found. She carried on with married men and spent a lot of time at the casino in Connecticut. Gambling was clearly a problem. Sarah recalled a time when she had to retrieve something from the trunk of Cathee's car and found more than a thousand lottery tickets, already scratched off.

I couldn't believe how poorly Cathee cared for her children. She gave me up because she had no money to take care of me, but when she had more than enough money, she didn't use it to take care of her other kids. Both Sarah and Lana struggled emotionally as they tried to tell me about Cathee. They said again how happy they were that I was raised by loving parents, and that it was probably for the best because Cathee just wasn't a very good mother in the end. I know they were trying to make me feel better about Cathee leaving me behind, but I didn't. I felt angry that Cathee wasn't there to tell me herself. I heard what they were trying to tell me, but only years later did I understand and agree with them.

I remember looking around the restaurant as we sat there enjoying our visit, thinking that the other guests had no clue how special this dinner was and how it would play out for each of us the rest of our lives. I found myself wishing that my daughter Samantha could have been there too. Sarah and Lana would have loved getting to know her.

I noticed that Lana hadn't had much at all to drink. Sarah and I probably drank the most. Although we weren't slushy drunk, we were buzzed. The cold walk back to our hotel sobered us up.

We stopped for a nightcap in the hotel bar, where Sarah told us about Lana's fantastic voice. After Sarah begged Lana to sing for us, she did "Killing Me Softly" a cappella. I was so happy to hear my talented sister sing! She said again that she wanted to pursue a career in music. I was so proud that she has this amazing talent.

Sasha and I said our good-nights and hopped on the elevator. Once the doors shut, we looked at each other, speechless. We knew exactly what the other was thinking: Sarah and Lana were absolutely wonderful. They were very proper and had good manners, but they were lots of fun to party with. As we lay in bed, I chattered on about the evening long after Sasha drifted off. It took me a long time to fall asleep.

The next morning Sasha and I met up with Sarah and Lana to go the Holocaust Memorial Museum. Sasha had studied the Holocaust in high school and wanted very much to visit this place. At the entrance, each of us randomly selected an identification card that told the story of a Holocaust victim. The idea was that you substitute your name and place of birth for that of the victim. Halfway through the museum I realized that the woman whose name I had selected was the fourth sibling in a family of nine—just like Cathee. It was painful to learn how horribly the Jews suffered during this tragic time in history, yet the experience allowed me to start relating to Cathee as part of a family—my family. The hardships and horrors the Jews experienced were vast, but maybe subconsciously I was hoping it would make us feel that much more grateful for the happiness we had in our own lives.

We rode the Metro to a mall and spent the afternoon shopping and exploring our nation's capital. It was too cold to visit too many monuments. I had seen them many times, but Sasha hadn't, and I wanted her to see my favorites: the Lincoln Memorial, the Jefferson Memorial, the Washington Monument, and the Vietnam Memorial.

The first time I visited DC, back before Sarah located me, I walked up and down the Vietnam Memorial, wondering if my birth father had joined the Army before I was born. My genetic history from Catholic Charities said he might have, but I never did get the feeling that he had been in the Vietnam War. Years later I would learn that he had tried to enlist but never served.

That evening Sarah's husband, David, drove down from New York to visit a friend in Alexandria. We all went to dinner at an Italian restaurant in Georgetown. Lana and Sasha both commented on how much Sarah and I had the same eyes. I think David made the same observation. It touched my heart to finally know that I shared some physical characteristic with someone other than my own children. It seemed to validate my existence as a blood relative, my genetic connection to a family.

Everyone was scheduled to leave the following day, Sunday. Sasha said her good-byes that night because she was flying out of Reagan National early the next morning. Lana also left early because she had to work later the next day. I missed giving her one more hug in the morning. After I checked out of the hotel, I hung out in Sarah and David's room, trying to squeeze in every last bit of conversation we could.

Sarah came down to the curb with me as I hailed a cab to the airport. While the driver loaded my luggage into the trunk, she and I gave each other a hug and started to cry. I didn't want to let her go. We both felt the love for one another that had been absent for so many years. I remember waving and pressing my hand against the window as Sarah skipped along the sidewalk as the cab pulled away, looking like she probably had when she was a little girl. She waved until we drove out of sight. I remember telling the driver, "That's my little sister."

I closed my eyes, trying to press back tears that insisted on falling.

I felt so grateful. After years of being apart, Sarah chose to search for me and to make me a part of her life. She took a chance that I wanted to be found as well. If she hadn't, I'd still be trying to fake how happy I was on my birthdays when deep inside they only reminded me that no one in my birth family cared enough to find me. There were no guarantees that future reunions would go as smoothly, but for the moment I felt deliriously happy.

CHAPTER 10

Tommy's Children

During that same trip to DC in January 2003, I periodically called my office for phone messages. One of those messages held yet another surprise. I believe the coworker who read it to me was aware of my reunion situation, but she still sounded a little uneasy relaying the words to me. The message said: "Susan, I knew all about you and want to talk as soon as possible. Please call me. Love, Aunt Evie."

The karma of that weekend sure was working! I told my coworker that she had no idea how much that message meant to me, how big a mountain it moved for me. Evie Conklin Shew was the half-sister of Tommy Conklin, my birth father. I'd been hoping she'd call. She held the missing pieces to the puzzle of my life.

Since learning my birth father's name, I had been trying to track him down through the tribal enrollment office at the White Earth Indian Reservation in northwestern Minnesota. I explained that I believed my birth father was a registered tribal member, but the enrollment clerk informed me that they just didn't randomly give out this sort of information. I pleaded with him, so he asked a few simple questions: What year was Tom Conklin born? I didn't know, but I told him that my birth mother was born in 1945, so Tom was probably a few months older than she was. He admitted that there was a registered tribal member by that name, and the date of birth was probably a good match, but the records showed that he was recently deceased, within the last year. My heart sank. How could it be that both of my birth parents were dead? All of the questions I'd had for so many years, questions I'd wanted to ask them face to face, would now have to be answered secondhand. I switched tacks. I told the clerk that I was hoping to locate whatever siblings I might have through my birth father. Was there a last known address for Tom? Yes, he replied. In Auburn, Kansas, just southwest of Topeka.

It didn't take long to find a phone listing for Tom Conklin, but I sat on it for a couple of days and talked it over with Eric Keene, my best friend and former coworker. Eric was also an adoptee; he now worked in Washington, DC. Eric warned me not to just pick up the phone and call Tom's widow and start babbling hysterically about being her dead husband's illegitimate child. Eric knew me pretty well. He was concerned I was going to shatter this woman's life if she already didn't know about me.

As much as I sympathized with my birth father's widow, I felt I had every right to contact whatever siblings I might have. I'd waited long enough to find my biological family. I wasn't going to tiptoe delicately because it might hurt somebody's feelings. My own feelings had been hurt by years of silence.

The woman who answered the phone verified that she was Linda Conklin, Mrs. Tom Conklin. Just as Eric predicted, I started babbling. But I did it in a way that felt right. I explained that I was an adoptee and had recently been told who my birth parents were. I told Linda I believed that my birth father was her late husband. She carefully listened but admitted that this was the first she had heard of it. Tom had never told her anything about having a child when he was a teenager. I pressed harder. I said that I knew Tom lived in Minnesota back in 1962 and came from the White Earth Reservation. He had a girlfriend named Cathee Dahmen, and Tom's half-brother, Jim, had dated one of Cathee's sisters (Elaine). Yes, she admitted, Tom was from Minnesota and did have a brother named Jim, but it still didn't seem to register.

Deep down inside she may not have wanted to believe me. But I felt sure that she must have known something about it. Tom couldn't have hidden this information from her for so many years. I told her that I understood a little of what she must be feeling. When I learned these details a few days ago, I was just as surprised as she was. I started crying. I told her I didn't mean to hurt her, but I had wondered for years who my biological parents were. Now that I knew both were dead, I wanted to reach out to my siblings.

She told me a bit about Tom's three children, all by his first marriage. She gave me their names, the cities they lived in, and their phone numbers. She said that between her three kids and Tom's three, they had eleven grandchildren. I asked how she was doing since Tom's passing, and we exchanged e-mail addresses. Before I hung up, I told her that I hoped I would talk with her again someday.

The conversation had gone well, or at least as well as it can when someone finds out their deceased spouse had an illegitimate child. But then I worried I might have crushed her idea of who her husband was. He had held his secret from her their entire married life.

It wasn't going to be a secret much longer. After Linda and I talked, she called Tom's half-sister Evie and asked, "Does the name Cathee Dahmen mean anything to you?" Evie told Linda that before he died—on January 7, 2002, almost one year ago to the day—Tom had confessed to her that he had had a daughter with Cathee. I'm not sure what other information Tom told Evie at the time of his confession. By then he was in hospice. But what he told her was all that really mattered.

It was at that point that I received Evie's message. We talked a while, and she also gave me the phone number for Tom's eldest son—my brother, Tom Jr. He wasn't home, so I left my name and hotel phone number with his wife and asked that Tom return my call.

The Conklin Kids

When Tom Jr. called back, I was a little taken aback to hear his deep Kansas accent on the other end of the line. I was expecting a Minnesota accent, I guess. (And yes, Minnesotans have accents just like everyone else!) I asked him whether Evie had broken the news to him about me. He said she had, and although I was a complete surprise to him and his brother and sister, I was accepted immediately. Tom Jr. was excited to talk with me and very kind. He told me that Tom Sr. had tried to tell him something shortly before he died, had struggled to get it out, but never succeeded. He was now certain that Tom Sr. had been trying to tell him about me.

Tom Conklin Jr and Tom Conklin Sr. Tom Jr's Wedding

I told Tom Jr. I'd also like to talk with my half-brother Jim and half-sister Emily Christine. Tom, who went by Junior, was the oldest of the three; he was thirty-five at the time. Jim (thirty-two) went by Jimbob, and Emily Christine (twenty-nine) went by Chrissy. (More nicknames to learn! Didn't anybody use their real names anymore?) I told Junior I would call them when I returned to Minnesota. I also told him that I was going to meet my half-sisters Sarah and Lana the next day. I told him how Sarah had found me and how nervous I was about the meeting.

After connecting with Tom Jr., we decided to meet, along with my other siblings on my birth father's side. We chose a weekend in May in Mahnomen, Minnesota, where my birth father had grown up. Evie and her husband, Elmer Shew, would drive from Oregon to Minnesota in their RV to meet us.

By now I knew a few basic facts about Thomas Leroy Conklin: He had been born March 13, 1944, at White Earth, Minnesota. He and his younger siblings—half-sister Evie & Kathy and half-brother Jim—had the same mother but different fathers. Tommy lived in foster care with Carl and Loretta Huset of Middle River, Minnesota. Tommy moved to Cleveland, Ohio, around 1964, where he met and married Nellie Cadue. After three children and nine years of marriage, they divorced. Tommy moved to Topeka, where he married Linda Smothers and worked at the Topeka Juvenile Correctional Facility for twenty-four years.

I found it ironic that my birth father spent a quarter century helping juvenile delinquents turn their lives around. Was this atonement for his own boyhood sins?

The Conklin Reunion

I was nervous the night before for my road trip to Mahnomen to meet the Conklins, so much so that I barely thought twice about making the five-hour drive by myself. I decided to take my 1978 Z28 Camaro, a birthday gift from Tim. It was a special occasion, so why not drive my special car?

I also asked my Aunt Elaine to join me. Elaine knew my birth father's family way back when. She had dated Jim, my birth dad's brother, and had known his sister, Evie. I knew Elaine would jump at the chance to drive up to the White Earth Indian Reservation. She could be a part of the reunion, but she would also have time with the slot machines.

I got off work late that Thursday afternoon, drove home to switch vehicles and pack up, and got back on the road before rush hour. I had knots in my stomach. In a few short hours, I would finally meet my siblings on my birth father's side. It wasn't long before I pulled off the road to buy a couple packs of smokes. That's what I did when I was nervous. I usually slipped into a convenience store to buy a pop and some gum and a pack of Marlboro Reds. I always feel like the clerk knows I'm doing something wrong, like he knows that I should know better, or that I'm sabotaging all those months it took me to quit.

I jumped back into the Z, rolled down the windows, and turned up the 8 track AM/FM radio. Soon my mind drifted back to meeting my three Conklin siblings, and I thought, *What will they look like? What will they be like? Will they accept me as their sister? Will I disappoint them?*

I came up alongside a train on a railroad track running parallel to the road. I tried to outrun the train and found myself going about seventy-five miles an hour. At first I was side by side with the train, and in just a short time, it was long behind me. Ahead I saw white clouds in a blue sky, smelled sweet clover grass, and heard crickets chirping.

I arrived a few hours earlier than my siblings. Their drive from Kansas would take at least eleven hours. I found Elaine in the hotel lounge, enjoying a beer and playing video poker. Prying her off her chair from a hot slot machine could be done, but only if it were a fire drill and I was a fireman. I sat next to her and asked the bartender for a Corona, then another. I could have easily tossed back a couple more beers. I was worried about the meeting not going well, and the beers took the edge off. But I didn't want to *appear* drunk and give them the wrong impression.

Elaine and I checked into our hotel room, a smoking room no less. I suddenly realized that for the first time in my life, I would be spending the night with my aunt. The sleepover was long overdue.

Because the Conklins were due any minute, we headed back to the entrance of the Shooting Star Casino. Every time the doors opened I turned my head and wondered, "Is it them?" After a while I noticed a woman sitting in a lounge chair with a perfect view of the casino entrance. She looked like someone I'd seen in a photo. I approached her and asked with a slight hesitation, "Evie?"

"Yes," she said softly with a warm smile.

Elaine joined us. She and Evie had known each other briefly in the 1960s, which made this meeting easier for me. There were the usual awkward moments and brief silences, of course. So many thoughts were running through my mind: *Does she think I look like Tom? What was it like to grow up with him? Was their relationship tender or annoying or both?*

Our conversation was abruptly halted when Evie said, "Here come the kids now." It seemed like all the slot machine noise stopped as I watched my brothers and sister walk into the casino. The moment I'd waited for was here. I gave Junior a hug, then Jimbob, then Chrissy. I hugged her longest, thinking about how we could have shared so many things that sisters do—chicken pox, first loves, clothes. We had so much catching up to do.

Susie meets the Conklin Siblings 2003   Chrissy/Susie/Jimbob/Cyrus/Tom Conklin Jr.

I knew they had to be tired from their long road trip, so we agreed to meet for dinner at the casino restaurant after they had a chance to check in and catch their breath. Elaine and I went back to our room to relax. It felt more like decompression to me. I had finally met my birth father's family, all the children that he recognized as his own. I wondered what life would have been like had we all grown up together. When I added and subtracted our differences, it all seemed to balance out. I was raised up north; they were raised on the plains. We don't have the same birth mother, but we share the same birth father. I was raised by adoptive parents; they were raised by biological parents. My adoptive parents are still married; their biological father divorced and remarried a woman with three kids of her own.

I had no history with them, and they had no history with me, yet I was their blood sibling, and they were mine. Tom Sr. clearly wanted it that way. Otherwise he would have told Tom Jr. the truth about me long before he was sick. Even so, I had to believe that every once in a while my birth father thought of me, but how often and when and with what level of guilt? What triggered those thoughts? Did he ever wonder what I looked like? If I was healthy? If I was even alive after all this time? Did he ever wonder who walked me down the aisle when I married the love of my life?

Over dinner with the Conklins, Elaine and I learned a bit more about their family. They had been raised in a traditional Native American home and community, going to powwows and enjoying their children as family's do. Chrissy was the vice chair of the Kickapoo tribe. Junior was the tribe's police chief. Although they didn't have a lot of money growing up, they said their father was always there for them. Still his marriage to Linda had put a strain on Tom's kids, who said they took a backseat to their stepmother's children.

Some years later, Nellie Cadue, Tom Conklin's first wife, wrote me a letter that supplied several details of my birth father's past. Nellie said that because Tommy's parents were alcoholics, he lived in foster care with Carl and Loretta Huset of Middle River, Minnesota. A Native American man whose last name was Smith but who claimed to be Tommy's father visited Tommy once after he moved to Cleveland, Ohio, with help from the Urban Indian Relocation Program. The program was funded by the Bureau of Indian Affairs and helped young Native American adults and young families move from their reservations to large US cities for an education and jobs. Tommy trained at the Cleveland Barber College.

Nellie and Tommy met, married, and had three children in Cleveland: Tom Jr. in July 1967, Jim in 1970, and Chrissy in December 1973. In 1974 the Conklins moved to Kansas to be closer to Nellie's family, who belonged to the Kickapoo tribe. Tommy learned construction skills through Kickapoo's on-the-job training program known as the Indian Action Team. He didn't like the work, and as problems developed in the marriage, Tom started drinking. After he and Nellie divorced in 1976, he moved to Topeka, where he married Linda Smothers and worked for the Topeka Juvenile Correctional Center. At one point, Tommy and Junior worked there together.

Tom Sr. was a smoker. When he was diagnosed with terminal cancer, his children went to be with him, despite their strained relationship with Linda. But not once in all that time did Tommy Conklin mention another child—to Nellie or Linda or to his children. He told only his sister, Evie, just before he died. When Tommy and Nellie's children found out, Nellie said, they accepted me as the older sister. "There was no hesitation," Nellie said, "just acceptance."

Thinking back now, my dinner with Tommy's other children seemed like any normal family reunion, except that this was our first reunion, not our tenth or twenty-fifth. I couldn't help but wonder what my birth father would think if he knew we were all together.

A person could go insane thinking about what might have been.

CHAPTER 11

White Earth Nation

One of the missions the Conklin clan and I had that weekend in May 2003 was to see if I could become an enrolled band member with the White Earth Indian Reservation. Minnesota has eleven Native American communities, seven that are Ojibwe (also known as Chippewa and Anishinabe), including the White Earth Nation. The White Earth Reservation, which is sixty-eight miles east of Fargo, Minnesota, was created in 1867, during President Andrew Johnson's administration. I vaguely remembered reading about the squabble over hunting and fishing rights that the White Earth Nation won back in 1981.

Junior, Jimbob, and Chrissy were members of the Kickapoo Indian Reservation in Kansas through Tom Sr.'s first wife, Nellie Cadue. But because Tom Sr. had been enrolled as a member of the White Earth Nation, it seemed fitting for me to be enrolled too. The Conklin sibs had drafted an affidavit confirming that I was their blood relative.

We met up again for breakfast in town before heading to the White Earth enrollment office. Evie and Elmer, plus Elaine and Cyrus, Jimbob's five-year-old son, came along.

I recognized the enrollment clerk as the guy who sang karaoke in the hotel bar the night before. All of us—my siblings and my aunts—worked patiently with him as he tried to compute my blood quantum and that of my birth father. The quantum amounts seemed wrong to

Evie. She finally realized that because she, Tom Sr., and their half-brother, Jim, had come to the "rez" from a foster family, the data was incorrectly listed on the enrollment records. That meant if Tom Sr.'s blood amount was wrong, so was mine. The minimum blood quantum for enrollment was one-quarter.

I thought I would be welcomed with open arms. Instead the path was blocked by miles of red tape. There would be no easy way to correct this question of blood relation, but we started the process anyway.

While we waited for the clerk to copy some of the paperwork we had brought in, I finally got the chance to talk to the Conklin siblings about Cathee. I had brought a few photos to share, and they voiced their approval of their father's choice of girlfriend back when he was a teen.

On our way back to the hotel, Elaine confessed that she would like me to get enrolled with the Grand Portage Band of Lake Superior Chippewa. She said it seemed right that I try to get enrolled with my birth mother's tribe. The idea of getting enrolled with either reservation seemed a little odd to me, since neither of my birth parents had acknowledged me and especially since I had always thought of myself as white, not Indian. It really didn't matter to me one way or another as long as I belonged somewhere. That's all I wanted—to *belong*.

On the last day of the weekend, the Conklins gathered for a picnic in the RV park where Aunt Evie and Uncle Elmer were staying. Evie had invited Conklin family members still living in the Mahnomen area to join us. Tom Sr.'s brother, Jim, wasn't there; he hadn't communicated with the family for years. Evie got a chance to catch up with family she hadn't seen in ages. I was so overwhelmed that the new names and faces didn't register.

My Conklin siblings were at least familiar with most of these people by name. Tom Sr. had brought the kids to Minnesota at least a couple of times during their childhood. But even they were overwhelmed by all the relatives. Since this was a family reunion, some of the relatives chatted with me as if I knew who they were. As I mingled, I found myself explaining that I was Tommy's older daughter. Some folks were caught off guard because they didn't recall that Tommy had four children, only three. They didn't ask about it, and I didn't explain.

I was so thankful that Auntie Elaine had met up with me in Mahnomen. Having her present while I was introduced to the Conklin family made me feel so comfortable. Besides, they all got to know and like her.

We took several photos, and then it was time for everyone to head home. I was amazed I made it back to the Twin Cities in one piece. My attention kept drifting away from the white lines of the road. So much had happened all at once and so fast that I couldn't absorb it. It was like an out-of-body experience. I was living it but not believing it.

After driving a few miles, I stopped at a McDonald's and found a spot in the parking lot where my mind could be still and soak it all in. I leaned back against the headrest and closed my eyes. I finally had the keys to open the doors to my past and my culture. It felt natural to want to know everything I could about being Native American. But I felt so confused, not only by my heritage but by my place in my new family order.

That weekend, for instance, I had learned from the Conklins that, according to native tradition, the eldest child was appointed to take care of family business. He or she was the one responsible for everything from financial decisions to burial wishes. I was now recognized as the eldest among Tom's children. Was Junior passing an invisible torch to me that weekend? Was I expected to take on these new responsibilities? Did I want to? Did I have a choice after all these years?

My mind filled with more questions. Was I white or Indian? Had I been lost or missing or left behind? Would I ever really feel like I knew Cathee or Tommy? I had more questions than answers, more doubts than reassurances. My only choices were to stay in the fog or walk out of it. I opened my eyes, turned on the ignition, and headed back to the only home I knew I could count on being real.

CHAPTER **12**

Grand Portage Nation

A couple of months later, in July 2003, I decided to follow Elaine's suggestion to try to get enrolled in the Grand Portage Band of Lake Superior Chippewa. The tribe was Cathee's; the reservation had been in existence since 1854, four years before Minnesota became a state. On my way up north, I'd also visit Cathee's final resting place. Some of her ashes were buried in a small Native American cemetery just north of Grand Marais. Some were with her other children. The rest were scattered. This trip would give me some much needed time to be in Cathee's presence, to talk to her, to comfort myself. I wasn't sure what I was going to tell her, but I'd figure it out once I got there.

I left on the afternoon of July 13, 2003, making good time on I-35. When I reached Grand Marias, I headed up Highway 61 along Lake Superior's north shore. The trip was just as beautiful as I remembered from my visit there with Tim the fall before. I stopped at Lakeside Cemetery just past St. Francis Xavier, a church built in 1895 by Jesuit missionaries for the Chippewa village. I began looking at headstones. The cemetery was so small that I figured it wouldn't take me long to find Cathee's grave, but I couldn't. By the time I read the last head-stone, I couldn't hold back the tears. *Even when I have all the correct information, I still can't seem to find her,* I thought. I was frustrated, sad, and angry. When I reached Grand Portage, I checked into my hotel room, buried my head in my pillow, and sobbed.

After I calmed down, I called Cathee's sister, my Aunt Barb, who lived in Grand Portage. Between sniffles I told her that I couldn't find Cathee's grave. She was surprised and said she'd help me find it that weekend. She then asked me to meet her at the Tribal Education Center, the place where the tribe's council members and administrators worked. Barb was working in the Energy Department for the tribe. She also wrote "The Moccasin," the monthly newsletter that was mailed to all the band members.

At the Tribal Education Center, the enrollment clerk recognized my name instantly. She told me that I was already enrolled as Susan Smith Fedorko and had been considered a long-lost member since 1992—five years before Cathee died. Both Barb and I were shocked. I was also elated. I had been enrolled for the last eleven years and never knew it! I silently thanked Cathee. I believed she must have had a hand in this. I had been learning about tribal customs and protocol, and there was one thing I knew for sure: only an immediate family member could get another family member enrolled.

The clerk also said that since I had been enrolled all those years, I was entitled to an accumulation of per capita money. Each year adult band members receive $1,800. For me, that added up to $19,800, plus interest. The clerk said she'd have to run the matter by the tribal chief, of course, who would confer with the other council members and then get back to me. I thanked her, and Aunt Barb and I left. Before we headed back to her office, we stepped outside to celebrate with a cigarette. While we puffed on our smokes, I noticed this handsome man walking our way. Aunt Barb introduced me to her nephew, Briand Morrison—the very same Briand Morrison who Cathee had babysat when she stayed with his father, artist George Morrison, in Rhode Island. That summer Briand was working for the tribe in the IT Department.

After meeting Briand, I was looking forward to being introduced to the many other cousins I would meet that weekend. In fact, Barb was planning a birthday feast in honor of her good friend, Lyle Sherer, and wanted me to be there to meet family and friends who were planning to drop by.

Cathee's Grave

The next morning we decided to make a run into Grand Marias to could pick up groceries. Along the way we stopped at the Chippewa City Cemetery where Cathee was buried. It was across Highway 61 from the cemetery at St. Francis Xavier, where I had looked the day before. I felt a little sheepish for searching as long as I did in the wrong place.

Aunt Barb walked with me to the Morrison/Dahmen graves and identified each one: my uncles George, Mike, Bernard and James; my grandmother Mary; my great-grandfather James Sr.; and finally, Cathee. Her grave had no headstone. Instead it was marked by a wooden cross, small and white and handmade by Roger Morrison, Mary's brother. Tears burned my eyes as I looked at that humble resting place.

I had planned to come here alone. I had wanted our first moment together to be just the two of us. So I spoke silently. "Sarah found me, Mom," I said. "I came home. But you're not here for me anymore. I guess we just keep missing each other. I love everyone, Mom, but I need your help. I don't think I'm as strong as you were. I wish you were here with me."

I realized that Barb had been talking to me while I was talking to Cathee. Barb fumbled for a cigarette in her purse, and for a moment I thought she was going to light up. Instead she broke open the cigarette, pulled out the tobacco, and held it in her palm. She handed me one and told me to do the same. Then she told me to sprinkle it on Cathee's grave as an offering.

Why on earth would I sprinkle Cathee's grave with the stuff that had killed her? Aunt Barb could tell I was confused. "This is the native way," she explained. "We sprinkle tobacco as an offering and say a little prayer." I opened my hand and let the tobacco fall over the grave. I felt like crying but held back because of Barb. I continued to talk to Cathee silently. I told her I would never understand why she gave me up. I blamed her for not being there for me. I told her I felt like I'd been thrown overboard and left to swim my way back into the family.

Barb wanted me to sprinkle tobacco on my grandmother's grave too, but I could not do it. I could not pretend to mourn her loss or embrace the spirit of the woman who may have sealed my fate by banishing me from my family of origin. Cathee had blamed Leo, my grandfather; I'd always blamed Mary. As I stood over her grave, I rejected her. *Look at the wonderful person I have become. I could have been one of those grand-daughters you were proud of. But you never wanted to know me. You turned your back on me. I'm going to do the same to you. You didn't exist for me in life. You certainly won't exist for me in death.*

I did not want Barb to see how I really felt. This was her mother too, after all, as well as Cathee's. I meant no disrespect to Barb. I held out my hand but sprinkled nothing over Mary Dahmen's grave. We left the cemetery and headed into Grand Marais to shop for Lyle's party.

Later that afternoon I met Lyle Sherer, the man Barb had lived with for several years. He had been the love of her life, probably one of the only men she had ever considered marrying. Lyle had known Cathee; she had visited his home and his family. He made the most of his birthday party, and I loved every minute of it.

I met several of my cousins that night too, including the children of my Aunt Darlene, who died six months after Cathee died. When Cathee was in the hospital in Princeton, Minnesota, Darlene was in the hospital in Minneapolis. Darlene was still hospitalized on November 28, the day of Cathee's funeral.

There were so many new faces, yet it seemed to me that we all looked alike. I listened to their many stories about Cathee and their fondest memories of her. I kept thinking that I didn't know who this woman was, that I was the only one who didn't know who Cathee was in life. I did not know her voice, her walk, her touch. I felt so isolated.

Rejection

Several weeks after I had visited the Grand Portage enrollment clerk, she called to tell me that the tribal council members had determined that my enrollment in 1992 was an error. I would be considered enrolled as of July 13, 2003, the day I entered their offices. Therefore, I would not be eligible for any retroactive per capita accumulation.

How could the tribe consider my original enrollment date an error? Surely they had the name of the person who enrolled me. Couldn't they check? My blood quantum was the same as it was the day I was born. In fact it should be a greater percentage than what had been recorded because Evie was certain that both her blood quantum and Tommy's had been incorrectly recorded. I demanded their ruling in writing. It took almost three months. The blood quantum had to be a quarter, pure or combined. I could enroll at one or the other reservation but not both.

Welcome home, I thought, fighting back tears of frustration. Cathee's immediate family had embraced me. Why not her tribe? Why would the council members think my blood quantum was any different in 2003 than it was in 1992? How could eleven people have made the same judgment in error?

I had heard that tribes were suspicious of newcomers. I could understand their reasons, but I didn't consider myself a newcomer. Since then, I've learned that many Native American adoptees who are searching for their identities and trying to get enrolled are treated like this. What an injustice. Some of us live in states where adoption records are closed. The Indian Child Welfare Act protects only those children born after 1978, not before. It was my birthright to enroll in my birth mother's band.

I was furious at Cathee. I blamed her for everything, from not being around to help me fight for my rights to causing this entire mess.

I had to let it go, at least for the moment. The Metallica "Summer Sanitarium" concert on July 27 was around the corner at the Minneapolis Metrodome, and my cousin Steven Standing Cloud (Elaine's son) and I were huge fans. I'd lost out on so much time with all of my cousins on both sides of my birth family that I was glad for some bonding time with him. I'd never had this kind of opportunity back in my twenties and thirties, my hardcore concert going years.

Attending this event with Steven felt like such a normal family outing. At the moment, normal sounded good.

He and I would hear Metallica again the following summer at their post concert book signing. For now I just wanted to shout out how happy I was to be with family.

CHAPTER **13**

Cathee's New York

In the late summer of 2003, I made plans to visit my Dahmen siblings again but this time in New York. It would be my first trip there, yet I'd felt a gravitating pull to that city for as long as I could remember. It just felt like home. I'm not sure why, but I now believe it's because of all of the family who had lived there for so many years. Cathee lived there in the late 1960s with illustrator Antonio Lopez, then again in the early 1980s with her second husband, Adam Merrick. Lana, Adam Jr., and Sarah all had lived there as well.

I flew in on Thursday, October 9. When I told my good friend Eric Keene about the trip, he decided to drive from Washington, DC, to meet up with me. Eric and I worked side by side in Minneapolis for a couple of years before he transferred out east. We took smoking breaks together, we experienced 9/11 together, and we were both adopted. There's almost nothing I didn't confide in Eric. He'd been through every minute (on the phone) of my birth family reunion with me. I thought that when I met up with my siblings again, it would be great if Eric could be there as well. Having someone around who knows me well comforts me during uncertain moments.

After landing at JFK, I grabbed my luggage, hailed a cab, and was off to Grand Central Station to meet up with Eric. Along the way I soaked in the sights of this crowded city. Commuters zipped close by in their cars, skyscrapers rose cheek by jowl from the sidewalks, even headstones in the cemeteries were just inches apart from each other. *The dead must be buried twelve deep here*, I thought! Car exhaust mingled with the smell of hot dogs. I was a city girl, but these were sights and smells I had never experienced.

As I waited for Eric outside of Grand Central, at least twenty people of various cultures walked by. I had been in New York for less than an hour and already felt its intensity. It was a vibrant city, even and especially at lunch time. I spotted Eric's car and hopped in when he stopped to pick me up. I had wanted to come to this city for so long, and here I was driving out of it already. I kept looking out the window at the scenery, the sky, the buildings, the cabs, the lights. There was so much to take in!

Eric and I chattered nonstop for the next hour until we reached White Plains, where Sarah and David lived. We were scheduled to have dinner at their place that evening. A few toll booths later, we were on our way to our hotel. I had fantasized about staying in the heart of the city, at the Waldorf or the Plaza, but I just could not afford it for several nights. This room was deeply discounted, thanks to David. We hung out in the lobby until David picked us up. I couldn't stop thinking about meeting my little brother, Adam. He and his girlfriend were on their way by train to White Plains. I was so excited to meet him. What would we have in common? Would we look alike? Would I still need to convince him that we were blood relatives? We had talked briefly on the phone, and now I was about to share an evening of getting to know him. I had shared these thoughts with Eric, who knew just how important it was to me to have Adam in my life after all these years.

Sarah met us at the door of her apartment, bubbly and full of energy. She'd been cooking up a storm, and the place smelled great. I could tell that she loved to entertain and had spent a great deal of time making things perfect. It felt wonderful to be able to give her a big hug again. I realized that I missed her more than I knew since our first meeting in DC nine months ago. The same blood coursesd through our veins and bonded us. I wished I lived closer to her and

David. I had missed out on so many years with everyone. Could I ever get to know them as well as I would like with visits just once a year?

I gave Sarah and David a couple of my "lucky nuts" from the walnut tree that grows in my front yard. In spring the blossoms evolve into hard nutshells, and by summer they grow into larger nuts. In the late summer, I try to raid the branches before the nuts drop to the ground, and the gray squirrels to scamper off with them. I gather about forty of the nuts, dry them out until the shells crack, and toss the shells. Then I give them my Native American blessing: I hold them in the palms of my hands, close my eyes, and ask the Lord to send peace, good health, and prosperity to the kind soul who will hold them next. It's corny, but it's heartfelt. I give the nuts to family and to very good friends. I have given all of my aunts and uncles a lucky nut. I have even sent one to a photographer that Cathee worked with. I'm hoping he didn't think I'm some kind of nut myself!

Friends and family who know me well know that I believe that the nuts bring good luck, maybe not every time but eventually. That's why I gave one to David and Sarah. I knew that they were hoping to have kids soon. Sarah wanted to be a mother so badly. I wanted her to keep it close by as it would bring them luck with getting pregnant. (They now have three children.) I hoped they wouldn't think of me as some kind of superstitious freak. This was just the sort of wacky behavior Cathee was capable of! She and I were alike when it came to these types of strange beliefs. I recalled Aunt Barb telling me that Cathee used to spend hours on her hands and knees looking for four-leaf clovers that she could sell as lucky mementos at the Grand Portage powwows.

Sarah's phone rang. It was Adam. He and his girlfriend were at the train station. David excused himself to pick them up. When they returned, Adam and I gave each other a good, long hug. I could still see traces of the little boy inside this tall and handsome man. I was so overwhelmed. Thank goodness Eric could be with me to help steady my nerves. Adam, on the other hand, seemed completely at ease, chattering about this and that throughout the delicious dinner. I don't know that we touched on anything sensitive or awkward. It all felt easy and right. Before I knew it, it was time for David to take Adam and his girlfriend back to the station to catch the last train out. We said our good-byes, gave each other hugs, and promised to keep in touch via e-mail. Over dishes, Sarah said she was surprised that Adam was so talkative. I was just happy that he was receptive to me.

I didn't want the evening to end. So when David returned, we all packed up to find a nice bar where we could dance and talk quietly. Both Sarah and I probably drank more than we should have, but it was a blast! David ended up driving Eric and me back to our hotel.

The Saturday morning sun was a bit too bright after a night of several Coronas, but Eric persisted that we get out and explore the beautifully quaint town of Stamford. He settled into a sports bar to watch the Chiefs game, while I found bargains at secondhand shops. I guessed that the variety of beautiful clothes were wardrobe rejects from the women of nearby Greenwich. I was starting to regret that I hadn't brought a bigger suitcase.

On Sunday Eric and I drove back into New York to explore Manhattan. I had my heart set on a horse-and-carriage ride in Central Park. After settling into the carriage, we managed to hit three bars along the way. A couple of blocks away from the park, I realized we were in front of Carnegie Hall. Cathee had lived in an apartment with Antonio above Carnegie Hall. I suddenly felt weird about being in New York City. This was Cathee's turf, her territory. I hadn't been welcome in her life here in New York City, so why was I trying to fit in now? Maybe it was the alcohol, but I felt Cathee's spirit there. She hadn't walked these sidewalks in years, but she was there. Just as I had known that the name of my birth father was not carved into the Vietnam War Memorial Wall. There are feelings I get that I can't explain and yet believe to be true with absolute certainty.

By now, after drinking our way to Central Park, I had to go to the bathroom. The carriage driver dropped us outside of the Plaza, and I ducked inside. It was by far the most exquisite hotel I had ever stepped foot in. I made my way to the ladies room, admiring the brilliant chandeliers and shop displays all the way. I spotted a beautiful, snow-white, plush terry robe, monogrammed over the breast with antique gold threading. I wanted that robe so much! As I entered the ladies room, I noticed a mother and her darling little daughters all dressed up in ruffled dresses, summer hats, and white gloves as if it were Easter Sunday. Was this just another afternoon for them or would they be back in jeans and T-shirts tomorrow afternoon? It made me think about the mother/daughter moments I had missed out on with Cathee.

We made our way to Times Square, where I shopped for a Yankees jersey and T-shirts for the girls. We had a bite to eat at a German pub and had a few more drinks after sampling several shot glasses of different lagers.

Next stop was Ground Zero. Eric and I had been working side by side when the World Trade Center was hit and watched the coverage on a pocket-size television I had at my desk. I could feel the sadness as soon as we stepped out of our cab. As Eric snapped photos in and around the grounds, I read memorial messages written for the victims by their loved ones, perhaps in hopes of reaching out to their spirits with final words of farewell. I fought back tears and felt glad that Eric and I were there together. It was almost as if we needed to heal together.

On Monday we met my sister Lana for lunch at a restaurant near a marina in Stamford. She looked incredible. Like Cathee, Lana was drop-dead gorgeous, free-spirited, and a professional model as well as a singer. I was so proud that she was my sister. I still get the feeling that she does not believe that I am her biological sister. I wished that we were closer. We stopped at the Bruce Museum in Greenwich, the perfect ending to a long weekend in New York. Some pieces on display came from the Andy Warhol collection. I couldn't help but think that some of Cathee's friends were close friends, or friends of friends, with Warhol. It seemed I could not turn a corner in New York without running into her ghost.

My flight home didn't leave till midafternoon, so we picked

Coney Island as our final destination before heading to the airport. It was Columbus Day, a warm October afternoon, perfect for a visit to the amusement park. We rode the famous Wonder Wheel. Eric hated heights, but I was having a blast rocking the carriage we were in. Eric was pissed at me; all the color was drained from his face. We played games in the arcade, and I had my fortune told by the ancient, coin-operated fortuneteller. We walked along the boardwalk and watched people fishing on the pier and playing chess. Hassidic Jews strolled along the waterfront, enjoying the holiday. The water sparkled as a crisp, cool breeze chilled my arms. I could feel fall in the Atlantic air, but it could not have been a more perfect day. I was happy that my last moments in New York were so peaceful.

And yet on my flight back to Minneapolis, as I felt the engines roar and lift me up out of the metropolis of New York, I was no longer happy. I gripped the armrests of my seat, trying to hold back tears that rolled off my cheeks. As inviting as New York seemed, I didn't feel welcome there. The city was Cathee's world, not mine. I was not part of it and had never been invited to be part of it. Cathee wasn't there for me, just as she wasn't there for me in life. I was jealous, seeing all of my siblings in their comfort zones that didn't include me. I never thought I would feel this way. I could not ignore or control my disappointment. At that point, I wasn't sure I wanted to go back to New York ever again.

All I could think about was getting home to Minnesota, where I could feel safe within my routines. Away from Carnegie Hall and Central Park, I could focus on weekends up north at the cabin, a regular work week, grocery shopping, cleaning house—all the stuff of everyday life. The truth was my dreams had not taken me far from where I grew up. It seemed there had always been an imaginary circle around the city of Minneapolis, and I'd traveled only within that circle. The truth was I'd just always been more comfortable staying close to home.

After listening to some of the highlights, Tim seemed almost happy that my trip hadn't gone the way I thought it would. All of the phone calls from the new family and all of the attention on the past drawing away from the present were creating a dividing line through our relationship.

There were times when he felt protective and times when he was curious, always seeming to be within earshot when I was talking on the phone with this sibling or that uncle. Other times he seemed jealous that this new family wanted to get to know me and have me in their lives. His question was: Did they want *him* in their family too? Or was it just me they were after? I believe he thought that I was beginning to need my birth family more than I needed him. "We'll be here when you're done with them," he once said.

I hadn't intended to isolate him or our girls from my discoveries or keep reminding them that I wasn't completely focused on them, but then I realized I was talking about nothing else. I worried that it was getting repetitive for him and others as I told them my story over and over again. Maybe he didn't always want to hear about every little detail of the things I was learning. Then I began to lose track of whether I had told him the latest news of the day. Finally I kept that news to myself, knowing that he didn't much care either way.

Finding my place in this world of many families has been a tug of war, with me in the middle between past and present, old and new, the known and unknown. It has not been an easy place to be.

CHAPTER 14

Rendezvous

On the second Thursday in August 2008, shortly before eleven o'clock, I left for Grand Portage and the weekend of the Great Rendezvous, hosted by the Grand Portage Lake Superior Band of Chippewa. Every Dahmen, Standing Cloud, and Morrison made an effort to gather at this annual celebration and powwow, where we'd catch up with family and friends, attend feasts, and try our luck at the casino.

The drive from Minneapolis to Grand Portage is long—five-and-a-half hours from Minnesota's City of Lakes to its Arrowhead Region—and often seems longer when I'm by myself. It can be a lonely drive too, but the solitude often gives me time to think about who I'll see at the rendezvous and what we'll talk about. On this particular trip, I was content to listen to music. I'm not much of a singer, but when I'm alone I screech at the top of my lungs (with the lungs I have left) and nobody knows.

I enter the outskirts of Duluth, happy it was not a Friday, when every Twin Citian with a boat or an all-terrain vehicle always head up north along Highway 35. Duluth is always abuzz with sounds of road construction and eighteen-wheeler trucks downshifting on the steep hill into downtown. Before I descend, I can always can see the Aerial Lift Bridge and all the barges and container vessels anchored in the harbor. Even in August the water is cold—fifty-nine degrees on average—and you can stand in it barefoot for only so long. The shoreline view is always breathtaking. The color of the water should be marketed as Lake Superior Blue. I am comforted knowing that the lake will accompany me on my drive for the next two hours. Seeing it mile after mile gives you great respect for all the people who have worked on the boats of Lake Superior. So many men and women have perished over the years in these townships along the north shore, just trying to make a living. Gordon Lightfoot's "Gales of November" pops into my mind as I drive along the water's edge.

As I passed the haunting Glensheen Mansion, famous for the murder of its mistress and her nurse back in 1977, I couldn't help but steal several quick glances as I drove by. As I followed Highway 61 out of Duluth, I yearned to stop at the antiques stores and ice cream shops but managed to resist the temptation.

I passed Knife River, Two Harbors, Castle Danger, Beaver Bay, Silver Bay, Little Marais Cut Face, Grand Marais, and Five-Mile Rock. Thirty miles later I arrived at Grand Portage. This was God's country, and my soul was baptized with each sight. Did others travelers feel the same way? Did they realize that seeing these views is a gift?

I had made my way to Rendezvous Days more than a few times by now. After my birth family found me, my Aunt Elaine asked me to join the Dahmen/Morrison family at the tribal powwow. That was back in 2003. The problem was that the Northome County Fair was also held the second week in August. For the last twenty-plus years, Tim and I had gone to the fair. At least six of those years were continuous runs in the demolition derby. But back in August 2003, I convinced myself that going to Grand Portage instead of the fair was the right thing to do. I told myself (and Tim) that we had been following the same calendar of activities year after year, and that it was not only okay but important that I go to Grand Portage to be with the other side of my family. It wasn't an easy decision. I felt guilty that I wasn't spending that weekend in Northome at my parents' cabin as I had done for so many years. I knew how heartbroken they would be if they knew where I was going instead. I felt I was letting them down after all their years of raising me, and now I was trying to belong somewhere else. I worried that I might not have the opportunity to spend that special weekend with them next year if something should happen to them before then.

Rendezvous Days was one of the busiest, if not the busiest, weekends for the tribe. To get a room at the hotel lodge, you had to book it a year ahead. Many rooms had standing reservations. Back in 2003 Elaine gave me one of her three reserved rooms, so I could see what the powwow was all about. That was the summer I had visited the reservation for the first time, when I had tried to get enrolled with the tribe. So when I returned a month later for the rendezvous, I knew my way around the rez a bit. I knew where the powwow grounds were. But I was nervous because I was going to be meeting so many cousins. I could be walking right by them on the powwow grounds and have no clue we were related. I felt more comfortable at the casino. That's where I had spent much of my time, playing the slot machines, waiting until it was time for the Grand Entry.

Elaine told me that she usually got goose bumps when she attended the Grand Entry. That's when the arena crowd watched the presentation of the flags and staffs of the host tribe and guest tribes. Tribal elders, color guards, royalty, and dignitaries paraded in, followed by traditional dancers from oldest to youngest, moving to the beat of the drums until they circled the center of the arena to offer a prayer song.

After driving up for that first rendezvous, the trip in 2008 seemed easy. I could see why Elaine always talked about loving the drive. How I wished she were with me now. Elaine had been there to hold my hand throughout the reunion process, and I wasn't ready to lose her when she died on November 4, 2006, of brain cancer. I will miss her always and cherish the few times we did have together. It comforts me to think that she is in the spirit world with my birth mother, talking about everything Elaine and I had ever talked about.

I was so happy that Tim and Sasha wanted to attend Elaine's service with me. It was held at All Nations Indian Church in Minneapolis, the same church where Cathee's services were held. Later Elaine was given a traditional Native American burial with drums. Everyone did a wonderful job honoring her life, yet I couldn't help thinking, *Who am*

I going to talk to now about being accepted into the family? How am I going to fit in now? I was, in fact, already part of the family. I just didn't know it.

I spotted the sign for the Grand Portage Indian Reservation and crossed the invisible line that marked the divide between the rez and the rest of Minnesota. This reservation, my reservation, was established in 1854, and was known more than a century before that by the fur traders, voyageurs, and Indians who met there and traded goods with one another.

Every time I am in Grand Portage, I always make time to take the hiking trail to the "witch tree." This tree is known as "Manido Gizhigans" to the Ojibwe people. This beautiful four hundred-year-old sacred tree is perched along the rocky shoreline of Lake Superior. It stands prominently overlooking the lake and is considered a sacred area. Access to the tree is restricted to Grand Portage Band members only. I can feel the tree's power within me as it stands keeping watch over the lake.

Witch Tree – Little Cedar Spirit Tree – Grand Portage, MN
Photo by Travis Novitsky

I checked in at the front desk of the Hollow Rock Resort. Tonight I was staying in Cabin three, which overlooked Lake Superior and the Hollow Rock itself. The rock sits back a ways from shore, about thirty feet, and is about the size of a school bus. The waters of Lake Superior have washed against it every summer and winter for centuries. The shoreline lacks sand, which means it lacks a beach; instead it's littered with shale.

The cabins were about two miles down the road from the main hotel and casino, which is where I'd stay Thursday night, the only night I could get a room there on rendezvous weekend.

The cabins were cozy, each outfitted with a full kitchen, a bathroom with a tub and shower, and a heater. The TV played movies; it received no local broadcasts. I was much happier staying here at the cabin which is about 5 miles from the lodge/casino. It was isolated and away from the noisy slot machines, not to mention cigarette smoke, which aggravated my constant cough. By the time March rolls around each year, I am lucky if I can get through a couple of sentences without starting to cough. I've had this cough for so long, I know which time of year is worse for me and which is better. August is always on my side and not just for the cool evenings. The night sky was bright with stars. I was once told by an Ojibwe man that the stars were our ancestors whom we have lost to death. In looking at the skies that night in Grand Portage, there were many ancestors overhead.

I had no luck at the slot machines, so I wandered into the hotel bar where I immediately saw Aunt Barb and Darlene's kids: my cousins Lisa, Kathy, and Lori. I stayed up and had a few Coronas with them, then went to my room to bed. The next morning (Friday), I ate breakfast on my own at the hotel restaurant and watched the sun glisten off Superior's waters before heading back to Hollow Rock. Just sitting in the lodge on the reservation made me feel like I was part of the lifestyle I missed as a kid. Within the perimeter of the rez, I wasn't Susie but Cricket.

I bumped into one of my favorite uncles, Elaine's husband, Jim.

He referred to himself as the "white uncle." Uncle Jim had not been quite the same since Elaine's death. He was sitting with a tiny woman wearing men's navy blue slippers that appeared to be two sizes too big for her. Aunt Itzy—aka Barbara Morrison—was the younger sister of George, Roger, and Mary Morrison. She looked to be almost ninety pounds and short, with long, grayish hair pinned back with bobby pins. She didn't appear to be wearing makeup, except for a brush of pinkish rouge on her cheeks. She had a large purse in her lap.

Aunt Itzy – aka Barbara Morrison Capps, Susie's Great Aunt

Jim was determined that I meet Itzy because she lived in Clarksville, Tennessee, and didn't often come home. She had made it here a few years ago, but I didn't get the opportunity to meet her.

Once again I felt like I had to convince someone that I was Cathee Dahmen's daughter. My appearance took people here by surprise; I was so much heavier than my birth mother ever was. I could see them calculate the comparison in their eyes, or maybe I was just being hard on myself. The three of us talked about Cathee's life, Elaine's life, and how often Itzy came to Grand Portage. She asked about my job, my children, my husband—simple questions two people trying to get to know each other might ask.

Itzy told me that Grandmother Mary was superstitious; she never wanted to enter the house through the back door, for instance. Itzy asked if I was superstitious. I told her that in a way I was, that I did have my beliefs. Itzy told me that she did not consider herself superstitious, but she did carry around a good luck charm and had for years. She fumbled inside her purse and pulled out a shiny buckeye, same as my lucky nut! How remarkable that two relatives who had been apart for more than forty-six years should share the same belief in a lucky charm.

Aunt Itzy and I spent the rest of the day together. I drove her over to the powwow grounds and helped her get around. Her brother, Roger, often operated a moose burger stand at the powwow. He served the best moose burger at the powwow and had for many years. Itzy and I sat in lawn chairs near Roger's stand and visited with people who came up to talk to her. Many people were surprised that she was in Grand Portage. As I sat there next to her, nobody could tell that I had been absent from the family for as many years as I had. It was like I had been around for years and had taken on a role within the family and never knew it. I was the only child of Cathee's who lived in Minnesota like the rest of her birth family.

Aunt Itzy tired very easily, so I dropped her off back at the hotel lodge and casino. I didn't realize how frail she really was. This did not hold her back from lighting up a cigarette several times during the day.

The hold that cigarettes has had on this family is unbelievable. When Sarah found me, I was smoking a pack of Marlboro Reds a day. I didn't inhale, but I could feel the damage to my lungs, which were already affected by a lifetime of smoking. Sometimes I struggle so hard to breathe that I have a hard time exercising the way I would like to. I avoid bonfires completely. I'm cautious about using aerosol sprays of any kind.

Knowing how smoking has taken many lives within the Dahmen

family, I have quit, although I sneak a cigarette every now and then, usually when I drink a bit too much. I also enjoy a few smokes when I'm at the casino. I think Elaine's letter gives me permission to be "foolish"—to sit and smoke and come alive, just like she and Cathee did.

I miss smoking, but I want to live longer than Cathee did. She was fifty-two, much too young, when she died. She didn't live long enough to reunite with her firstborn or to meet her grandchildren. I want to be here when my girls marry and have families of their own.

The next day, Sunday, I woke up in my little cabin at Hollow Rock. I drove a little farther north to the lodge and casino for breakfast again. I met back up with Itzy, and we spent most of the day together. In the afternoon, she asked if I would drive her back out to Hollow Rock because the families used to gather there a lot for picnics. I thought that would be a great idea because she could look at the many hundreds of photos that I had of Cathee on my laptop. She had seen only a few that her sister Mary (Cathee's Mom) had sent her.

We sat in the sun, looking out over the lake from Adirondack chairs on the deck just outside the front door of my cabin. We talked for a couple of hours about the family in the old days: what life was like for her and her siblings growing up—the cold winters, school life, the family's struggles, their Catholic upbringing. She'd been quite the drinker in her day, she said, but she no longer drank. She described meeting her husband, Roy, how he didn't make the trip with her this year because he wasn't feeling well, and what her plans would be for a return visit to Grand Portage.

As I drove Itzy back to the lodge, I felt blessed to have spent the day with her, to have shared so much of myself, and to have had her share her insights with me. Meeting her helped me to reclaim my position within the Morrison/Dahmen family and to forgive the people I needed to. If her mother—my grandmother—had even an ounce of Itzy's character, maybe I could learn to love Mary after all. Before we said good-bye, she gave me a small, wooden, cutout birdhouse that she had picked up in a store along the way up to Grand Portage.

Aunt Itzy died three months later, just four weeks after her husband's death. I was shocked by her passing, but I was comforted knowing that she was with her family in the spirit world, catching up with them and visiting, just as we did at the Great Rendezvous.

Aftermath

When Sarah found me ten years ago, the anchor that had kept me grounded to a familiar and comforting place for forty years came loose and set me adrift. These days I'm never quite sure which direction life will take me. It seems that I'm always learning something new or different about myself and my birth families. There's no chart to guide me. There's no choice but to go with the flow.

Back when I was eighteen and searching for my biological family, I had endless questions about who I was. I knew I wouldn't feel complete until I knew the answers. Being young, I expected that putting the missing pieces of my life's puzzle together would be easy or at least not so hard. Now that I'm older, I wonder if I'll ever find the answers I've been looking for. In the decade since I was found, I've realized that facts aren't necessarily answers. The facts can tell you *what,* but they don't always tell you *why.* And facts change, depending on who's interpreting them. It's human nature to filter reality through our own perspective.

Not being able to talk with my birth mother or father or with my birth grandparents has been my biggest roadblock in finding one version of my life's story that's closest to the truth. When I started looking for my birth parents, I knew I might not find either of them. What I didn't expect was that both would be dead by the time I learned their names. I feel sad that they left no letters for me, no words of comfort, no explanation or apology. I guess I never really expected any messages from my birth father. The fact that Tommy told his sister about me shortly before he died is validation of my existence. But why did he wait so long? Up until then, he didn't acknowledge me, his first child. He didn't seem to want or need to know anything about me or Cathee. Did he still care about her? Did he know how successful she had become? Did he see her face on magazines while standing in line at the grocery store?

I will always want to know why Tommy abandoned Cathee. Why wasn't he there for her when she needed him? The simplest answer, I suppose, is that he was scared. He was just eighteen when I was born, but I can't help thinking he could have manned up and accepted his responsibilities. Within five years of my birth, after all, he was married and starting a family. Could he have matured that much in such a short time?

When I think that I'll never talk with Cathee and get the answers I have always dreamed of knowing, I feel especially cheated. I go back and forth about how I feel about her. It's like having a bad angel on one shoulder and a good angel on the other. The good angel rarely talks to me, but when she does, she gently reminds me that I was conceived out of the passion and poor judgment of two teenagers. They were probably ashamed at the way I came into their lives, and that's why I was given up. Then the bad angel goads me, reminding me that all of Cathee's older sisters had children out of wedlock. Other babies had been shuffled among various members of the Dahmen family to be cared for. Even Cathee's mother had had a baby before she married Cathee's father. Why was I the only one who was cast out? Then the good angel says that maybe I've obsessed too much about being the only family member who was banished. Maybe supporting one more unwed daughter was more than my grandmother could bear. Maybe she didn't want one more daughter to settle for less in life than she deserved.

I've decided that I should try to forgive my Grandmother Mary. Even if she *was* the one who packed me off to the adoption agency without Cathee's knowledge, she may be responsible for my chance at a better life than her daughter could have given me.

But it's not been easy for me to forgive my birth parents, especially Cathee. Truth is I'll never know whether she herself gave me up. I'll never know what she was thinking and feeling in our last minutes together. Did she feel angry or relieved? Years later, when I finally had the chance to talk with Dahmen family members about that, I got the feeling that Cathee knew deep down that my surrender was in my best interest and hers. Maybe that's why she never once tried to find me, at least not to my knowledge. And if she wanted to find me, she could have. She was the only one who had the resources to do so. In November 2006, when my Aunt Elaine was dying of brain cancer, I wanted to lean over and whisper into her ear, "Tell Cathee I forgive her." I just could not bring myself to do it. I've replayed that thought over and over in my mind in hopes that Cathee's spirit could hear me.

I've come to believe that I was found after Cathee died because she knew I would not easily forgive her while she was alive, and she could not face that. I feel her spirit, and I don't think her spirit is at peace. I believe her penance will be listening to me for the rest of my life without being able to respond.

The fact is I can never know first hand who my birth mother and birth father were and what made them tick. I can get close to their emotions and thoughts only through the people who knew them best. I have heard some stories from Adam Merrick, Cathee's second husband. In one e-mail he mentioned that Cathee would gaze off into space when she drank too much. Only then did she talk with him about me. In those vulnerable moments, did Cathee yearn to know what happened to me? Did her heart ache, never knowing my whereabouts?

Apparently her heart *was* broken in those first months after she moved to Rhode Island, according to Lou Mendelsohn, a trading software guru and my mother's confidante during her years in Providence. Lou contacted me in 2006 from his home in Tampa, Florida; he found me after searching for Cathee on the Internet and learning she had died. The last time Lou saw Cathee was in November 1965, during his Thanksgiving break from Carnegie Mellon University. He told me that he and Cathee had been very close and classmates, and that she had shared with him all of her heartache over losing me. He described how distraught she was that I was surrendered to the county. Lou has reassured me that Cathee loved me and spoke often of me to him. He says my voice reminds him of hers: soft and innocent, like that of a young girl.

I'll always feel that I missed out on something by not being a part of my birth parents' lives. Despite it all, I'm proud of them. Both were judged well by their peers. Both were held in high regard in their professions. Both had other children who enhanced their lives and felt love in return. I can't help but feel fortunate that I was raised as I was. I was placed into a family that loved me from the moment I arrived. I had a happy childhood; I felt nurtured and educated. I may look and sound and walk like my birth mother, but I was raised with the beliefs of my adoptive mother, who has influenced me most in my life.

I'll never know how my life might have turned out if Cathee had raised me, but if she had somehow found me after I had been adopted and tried to take me back, I would have been devastated to leave my adoptive family. I have never felt that I was not meant to be part of the Smith family. They are the ones who molded me into the person I am today. I have learned all my morals and values, mannerisms and kindnesses, habits and sense of pride from the Smiths. They have never once let me down.

I was an exception. Not all native children who are placed with "white" families have such happy lives. I belong to a network of Native American adoptees and fosters, some of whom have told horrific tales of being neglected and beaten by their white families and abused both mentally and sexually. My heart crumbles when I hear their stories. I'm often reminded that my own fate might have been the same as theirs. Instead the Smiths and I turned out to be a perfect match.

Reuniting with my birth families has had its ups and downs, the ups being all of the wonderful relatives I've spent time getting to know. Throughout the first year, I found that I was talking with some member of the Dahmen family daily. I talked with Aunt Elaine and Aunt Barb at least a couple of times a week, and I talked with Uncle Mike even more frequently. I still talk with my Uncle Mike at least once a week. I could talk with him for hours about everything and nothing. I think he really understands me.

I've had ongoing phone conversations with all of my newfound siblings as well. Still I wish I were closer to each of them. I wish we could have been part of each other's lives growing up. They sometimes seem to have little need for me in their adult lives. Maybe they're just set in their ways. Maybe I've been too pushy in my eagerness for details. I admit I am somewhat persistent when it comes to relationships. That's when I want to scream, "But I've been waiting for more than forty years!"

Other moments in this reunion process have hurt like hell. Take my falling out with my half-brother on my father's side, Tom Conklin Jr. I instantly fell in love with him and his entire family, including his wife, Miriam, and their daughters. I loved receiving her e-mails and photos of their girls. We bonded as sisters do, and she meant the world to me. But after she and Junior divorced, he quit corresponding with me for staying in touch with her.

I was angry with him for cutting me out of his life, but what hurt the most was that he would have nothing to do with my daughters either. I thought he was mirroring my birth father's actions with me. I felt abandoned, and the self-righteous side of me put an end to the relationship like water on a fire.

Anger turned to sorrow when I learned Junior had died in a car crash on July 10, 2009. I flew to Kansas to attend his funeral. The Horton Community Center parking lot was still packed when I arrived at the Kickapoo Reservation just after midnight. The all-night wake had begun at 8:00 p.m. According to the teachings of Chief Kennekuk, the nineteenth-century Kickapoo prophet, the men (plus Junior's mother, Nellie, and his aunts) would keep watch over Tom till dawn.

I saw JimBob and Chrissy from across the room. They greeted me with long, hard hugs, then Chrissy walked with me to Junior's casket.

His face was bruised, and he was dressed in his native regalia. He looked smaller than I remembered. Silently I told him how sorry I was about our last words.

The service began at 10:00 a.m. the next day after the grave diggers had prepared the burial site. The men sang several rounds of prayer and song until the feast began for the family and community. Everyone lined up to say good-bye to Junior, except women who were pregnant (the unborn are forbidden to greet the dead) and people wearing glasses (the dead must not face their own reflection; every mirror in the community was covered). After the shaman closed Junior's casket, his fellow tribal police officers carried his casket to his work truck while members of police departments from neighboring counties and states lined up behind it, their red lights flashing out of respect.

At the cemetery, after the shaman's final prayers, everyone turned to the east and silently offered prayers that would greet Junior on his first morning alone. A "last call" from the police dispatcher began with Junior's badge number: "Officer 84, come back. Do you have a copy?" He repeated the call until we heard, "Officer 84 is now patrolling the heavens." I couldn't take my eyes off Junior's three young daughters who were crying. Each person took a fistful of dirt and tossed it on his casket. Never once did I feel that I did not belong with the family as I sat with them that day. I felt only the sadness of his loss.

A couple of years after Junior died, his mother wrote me a letter, explaining that he had felt betrayed by my friendship with his ex-wife. She also said that he had sorted out all of those negative emotions before he died and had been talking about connecting with me again.

There have been painful dramas in the Smith family as well. My relationship with my parents has become strained as they have aged. Mom is ninety now and Dad is ninety-two. When Mom fractured a vertebrae in June 2009, she tried to suffer through it for several weeks while staying in Northome. That's when she and my dad realized they could no longer manage living in their dream home, and my sister Connie arranged for them to move into a Catholic senior complex in a Minneapolis suburb, one that would take care of their daily living needs.

This had to have been one of the saddest times in their lives. Not only were they leaving the home they had known for thirty-plus years, they were losing their independence. Mom would never again be able to weed her beautiful garden. Dad would no longer tinker around in his workshop. They had to pick and choose which pieces of furniture they would bring to their new apartment. With her bad back, Mom gave direction to Connie about what to keep and what to throw out.

When it came time to move, Mom rode to the Twin Cities with Connie. Tim drove the packed U-haul truck with Samantha as shotgun rider. Dad rode with me. The quiet life he and Mom had shared along the north shore of Island Lake had finally come to an end. I drove slowly along the shore road, letting him soak it all in, every last curve and driveway. I thought he might cry as we drove away, but he holds tight to his emotions.

My husband and I bought my parents' lake home *(Danola Lodge)* in January 2010, knowing how much my father wanted to keep it in the family. I was twelve when they bought it, and I and could not see them selling it to anyone else. I find the same joy that my mom did while weeding the garden and watching the lake's reflection on the ceilings. It is comforting to know that we now "own" the very place where Tim & I met. I hope that when my daughters inherit it, they will love it just as much and Tim and I do, especially when they hear the chorus of bullfrogs and the drone of mosquitoes at dusk, smell the damp carpet and moth balls at the end of a wet summer day, or see tree tips turning yellow and red and orange as they dance in the fall wind.

I have lived with my mother in my heart every day since she adopted me. I have admired her and have tried to mirror her selfless parenting, putting other family members' needs before my own. I have been blessed to have her in my life. She is my hero, and when she is gone, she will be my guiding star.

Since their move, however, my mother and father have seemed distant, no longer engaged in conversation. I've heard that it's normal for aging parents to become this way as they adjust to a less independent life. I keep telling myself that I'd be uncertain and depressed too if I were their age. I keep trying to put myself in their shoes. I can only imagine how worried they must be about their final days and how to prepare for losing one another.

Even so, it's heartbreaking to hear Mom say she is disappointed in me. I know she gets confused about information from me and information from my sister. That and other conflicts have led to a falling out with Connie. When I can, I always make time for my brother Steve and his family, and I am thankful that I have him for a brother. I keep positive and cherish the good memories I have with all the Smiths. Life is too short, and forgiveness and acceptance will eventually come. I have learned this from my relationship with my brother Tom Jr. Maybe someday I can find it within myself to draw Connie back into my life. For now I limit my communication with her.

Who Am I?

One of the hardest parts of having been found is having to answer to so many names and labels. Am I Susan, Susie, or Sue? Am I Veronica or Cricket? Am I a Smith or a Dahmen? Am I white or native? Am I Chippewa, Objiwe, or Anishinabe?

Early in my life, I think I realized that I was different from my friends, but I never really saw myself as a Native American before I was found. I saw myself the only way I knew how: as a Smith and as a white. When I was younger and looked at photos of myself, I saw a little white girl who looked scared but happy to finally have a home. Now when I look at myself in the mirror or look at photos of myself as a child, I see my Native American ancestry first.

I feel comfortable with what I have discovered about my native culture. I know I felt proud to attend the 2004 opening of the National Museum of the American Indian in Washington, DC, with my cousin Briand to see the art of his father, my great-uncle George Morrison, in the museum's inaugural exhibition. I've come to respect the land more after learning to embrace it better, especially when I hear my people talking about Mother Earth and the Creator. Going to the Grand Portage Rendezvous Days and Powwow every August brings me closer to my Morrison/Dahmen roots. It helps me to heal. It gives me inner peace. It allows me to accept what comes a little more easily. The ceremonial cleansing with sage calms me and comforts me. I have not yet danced at the powwows; I lack the courage it takes to do this anywhere other than in my own living room. Hopefully I'll feel confident someday and join my family in the circle.

Susie Fedorko May 2001

And then there's my name.

I've struggled all my life with my adopted name. I used to see "Susan Smith" as the sample name in those monogramming ads in magazines and the Sunday paper. It's always seemed so generic.

I've always been called Susie by the Smith family. The only time I was called Susan was by teachers in grade school or by the nurse at the doctor's office. I also call myself Susan at work and have for years. It's my legal name, and it fits me more professionally than Susie.

Tim's family have always called me Sue. I tried to correct this about two years into our marriage, but the name stuck. I admit that it's the name I like the least. I just think there are too many Sues in the world.

Most of my Conklin relatives call me Susie or Susan, mainly because that's the name they heard when I first surfaced. They have followed my lead in addressing me as Susan.

Veronica Rose is the name recorded on my original birth certificate. It's the first name I was given but the one I'm called the least. I love the name. I could be comfortable being called Veronica if I were called that every day.

Cathee called me Cricket when I lived with her, and that's the name the Dahmens have always used. It's all right with me, but the name drives my daughter Sam nuts. Tim too. He'll never accept people calling me by a name that's anything other than who he knows me to be. I find that the people who have known me the longest feel the most uneasy when I'm addressed by a different name.

It's exhausting and confusing, but I think I've grown comfortable with all of my names. I find that no matter what I'm called—Susan or Sue, Cricket or Susie—I take on that name's personality. Yet each personality is part of the other. I am all of these names, wrapped into one person. The name Cricket gives me a sense of who I might have been. I've taken on the persona of a much older, more responsible Cricket, one who hasn't experienced many hardships in life, who is stable and set in her ways, and who has structure in her life. This is true for the name Susan as well. Susan is shy but gets along well with most people at work. She puts her own needs aside so she'll have the energy to make others smile. She has worked hard for the things she has. She would do most anything for her family.

I am nothing less than grateful to have discovered all the details I have about myself. I'm still in awe of what I learn each day. Sometimes it's the small coincidences that mean the most. It was a surprise, for example, to realize that my adoptive mother and my birth mother have birthdays one day apart: Virginia on September 15, Cathee on September 16. I find it fitting that Virginia's birthday is first, as she is the mother who's first in my heart. Their birthday gemstone is the sapphire, which is my favorite birthstone color.

The little girl that I was seemed lost and wanted to belong. The woman I have become knows where she belongs and believes she was found just in time. I've met and become acclimated with my birth families, and when I suffer the loss of my adoptive parents, I know I won't be alone. Each of the people I know now, and all of the spirits I have met and lost along the way, have helped mold me into the woman I am today. Each has left an impression on me that will last until the day that I pass. Cathee was strong and accepted her fate in the end. I too feel strong and will follow her lead.

Each has left an impression on me. She's been gone fifteen-plus years now, yet I still feel the warmth of her spirit. In time I believe I'll be able to forgive her. I still get angry with her, and when I do, I drive like a mad woman into the city and park my car outside of the house I grew up in. I sit back and look at it, wishing I could go inside and upstairs to my old room. Does it still look the same inside? Do the stairs still creak when they're stepped upon? Do the windows still have my initials carved in them? What initials would I carve in them now? Who am I now?

I come back to the house to renew myself. Being there calms me and allows my doubts and stormy troubles to pass. When I leave, I feel revived, like a phoenix rising from the ashes. When I leave, I know that no matter what I am called, I am more than a name. No matter what I am called, I am a friend.

I am a cousin.

I am an aunt.

I am a sister.

I am a wife.

I am a mother.

I am a daughter.

I am a friend

No matter what I am called, I know I am loved.

Susie's saved concert ticket stubs
July 27, 2003 Metallica Concert with biological cousin Steven Standing Cloud
November 25th 1997 Rolling Stones Concert which was the day Cathee Dahmen
passed away.

Appendix A: Timeline

Mar 13, 1944   Susie's birth father, Thomas Leroy Conklin, is born in White Earth, Minnesota.

Sep 16, 1945   Susie's birth mother, Catherine Veronica Dahmen, born in Minneapolis to Mary (Morrison) Dahmen and Leo Dahmen.

July 1947   Lloyd and Virginia Smith, Susie's future adoptive parents, give birth to Stephen Smith, their first child.

1959   Lloyd and Virginia Smith adopt Connie Marie, Susie's older sister.

June 23, 1962   Veronica Rose Dahmen is born to Cathee Dahmen at St. Joseph's Hospital in St. Paul, Minnesota. Cathee is sixteen years old.

June 1962-June 1963   Cathee and Veronica live with Cathee's sister Marie Villebrun, and two kids in Minneapolis.

June 11, 1963	Veronica is surrendered to Commissioner of Public Welfare and placed in foster care.
Summer 1963	Cathee moves to Providence, Rhode Island, to live with Uncle George Morrison, a Native American expressionist artist, and his wife, Hazel, and their son, Briand.
March 13, 1964	Veronica Rose Dahmen becomes Susan Clare Smith when she is placed with Virginia and Lloyd Smith of Minneapolis.
April 12, 1965	Susie's adoption is finalized in Hennepin County, Minnesota. Tommy is relocated to Cleveland by the Urban Indian Relocation Program.
1966	Cathee graduates from high school and moves to New York City. She rooms with *New York Times* illustrator Antonio Lopez. Tommy Conklin marries Nellie Cadue.
1967	Susie starts kindergarten. Eileen Ford Agency signs Cathee; she is twenty-one years old. Tommy and Nellie Conklin have their first son, Tom Jr.
1970	Tommy and Nellie Conklin's second son, JimBob, is born.
1971	Cathee marries British actor Leroy Winter. Susie starts fourth grade.

1972	Susie starts fifth grade. Cathee gives birth to Sarah in Greater London, Middlesex.
1973	Tommy and Nellie Conklin's daughter, Chrissy, is born.
1974	The Conklin family moves to Kansas.
1975	Susie's parents buy former Danola Lodge in Northome, Minnesota.
1976	Susie starts ninth grade at Ramsey Junior High. Cathee turns thirty. Tommy and Nellie Conklin divorce; Tommy moves to Topeka.
1977	Susie starts tenth grade. Cathee divorces Leroy Winter and marries musician Adam Merrick in London.
1978	Cathee gives birth to Lana.
1979	Tommy Conklin marries Linda Sommers.
1980	Cathee gives birth to son Adam Jr.
1980	Susie graduates from Washburn High School, Minneapolis. Cathee retires from modeling at age thirty-four.
Dec 1982	Susie, age 20, marries Tim Fedorko, age 23.
May 1983	Susie gives birth to daughter Samantha.

June 1985	Susie gives birth to daughter Sasha.
1986	Cathee turns forty.
1987	Cathee moves to Stamford, Connecticut.
1988	Susie and Tim's home in Burnsville, Minnesota, burns, a total loss.
1992	Cathee's father, Leo Dahmen, dies.
1996	Cathee turns fifty. She moves to Princeton, Minnesota.
1997	Cathee Dahmen dies in Princeton, Minnesota, of emphysema at age 52. Susie is at the Rolling Stones concert in Hubert Humphrey Metrodome.
2001	Cathee's mother, Mary Morrison Dahmen, dies.
January 7, 2002	Tom Conklin dies in Auburn, Kansas, of cancer at age 57.
November 25, 2002	Susie's half-sister Sarah calls; Susie is forty years old.
December 7, 2002	Susie meets Dahmen aunt and uncles.
January 9, 2003	Susie meets half sisters Sarah and Lana.
January 2003	Evie Conklin Shew, sister of Tom Conklin, calls Susie for the first time.

July 2003	Susie meets Conklin half-siblings Tom Jr., JimBob, and Chrissy. Susie tries to enroll in her birth father's tribe, then her birth mother's.
August 2003	Susie attends first Grand Portage powwow.
October 2003	Susie meets half-brother Adam Jr.
Spring 2004	Susie and Tim travel to Kansas to meet Linda Conklin, Tommy's second wife, and to visit Tommy's grave.
July 10, 2009	Susie's half brother Junior is killed in a car crash.
April 2012	Susie completes DNA testing with her Uncle Jim Dahmen, 94 percent probably match
June 2012	Susie Fedorko turns fifty.

Appendix B: Hangover Soup

My Aunt Barb gave me this recipe, which the Dahmen family is very proud of. They stand by it as a soup that will make you feel better if you have a hangover! You can make hangover soup two ways. The recipe below shows how I make it. I never measure anything, so try it to your liking.

Spaghetti noodles
1 lb. hamburger
Onions
Celery
1 medium can or two small cans tomato sauce
Salt
Pepper
Celery salt

Cook enough spaghetti (measure with your middle finger and thumb so they don't touch) in about 3 quarts of water. Don't drain. Fry hamburger, half a small onion, and three stalks (stems) of celery (should be cut up small). Cook until hamburger is done. When spaghetti noodles are done, throw in the hamburger mixture, tomato sauce, salt, pepper, and celery salt to taste. Let this cook for a little while (5 minutes?). The secret is to throw in the hamburger mixture with the grease! Add salt and pepper and celery salt so it tastes good to you.

CPSIA information can be obtained at www.ICGtesting.com
Printed in the USA
LVOW010517021212

309686LV00003B/454/P